Lou,

Best wishes for continued career success.

Take Control—

Tommy

07-06-07

"Excellent — a must read for anyone who does not get up in the morning excited about going to work. *The Mulling Factor* has identified one of the most unrecognized, unappreciated and unaddressed problems in the workplace today — misemployment — and provides a practical, understandable game plan to take charge of one's career."

— **Jim Coil**
Partner, Kilpatrick Stockton LLP

"*The Mulling Factor* is an indispensable tool kit for surviving and thriving in today's uncertain work environment. It gives the reader a very simple, unique approach to a subject that is anything but simplistic."

— **Bill Rhodes**
Senior VP, The Ritz-Carlton Hotel Company

"There is no substitute for understanding the key relationships in one's work world. Mulling has developed a tool that provides that understanding and the success and happiness that follows."

— **Hala Moddelmog**
President, Churchs Chicken

"A practical guide for getting it right — i.e., job choice, career survival, and life satisfaction.... As Emory says, getting past the 'snow job' to the 'right job' equips the astute professional with insight and assessment tools for finding that 'great match' between you and your job; importantly, Emory alerts us to the warning signals of a poor match and offers practical advice for coping with less than ideal working circumstances.... You should keep this book in a 'prime location' on your bookshelf throughout your career."

— **Patrick R. Dailey, Ph.D.**
Vice President of Human Resources, Lucent Technologies

"*The Mulling Factor* is more than just a book; it is an incredible tool used to discover your ideal boss and optimal work environment."

— **Mike Cather**
Former Major League Pitcher, St. Louis Cardinals

"Worn out, weighed down and plain old tired of working for the wrong people, in the wrong job or organization? *The Mulling Factor* is the one book that you need to read or give to a friend. The insights provided into understanding and finding the right career fit are spot on. You will be able to use 'the factor' to put your boss and your organization and yourself into the right alignment."

— **Bob Leyda**
Former Vice President of Human Resources, Lend Lease

"As a human resources executive, I have personally seen the positive results of the coaching skills of Emory Mulling. This is quite a gift to now have these guidelines in a book. Everyone who reads *The Mulling Factor* will be able to apply these principles and experience the benefits of valuable executive coaching."

— **Valerie Zaleski**
Vice President, Human Resources, AIG Aviation, Inc.

"This is a must read for all people looking for career revitalization. *The Mulling Factor* captures the essence of defining what it takes for someone to successfully manage his or her own career. [The book] offers sage counsel for anyone wishing to take a leadership role in their own career development. It is straightforward, practical, and extremely informative. This is a must read for anyone who faces one of life's most difficult tasks — career management. Most people spend more time planning their weekends than their career. *The Mulling Factor* offers those individuals who have not given their careers much thought an avenue to truly take charge of their own career direction."

— **Blake J. Geoghagan**
Partner, Deloitte Consulting

THE MULLING FACTOR

Get Your Life Back by Taking Control of Your Career

THE MULLING FACTOR

Get Your Life Back by Taking Control of Your Career

by Emory W. Mulling

PRESS

A Division of the Diogenes Consortium

SANFORD • FLORIDA

Published by DC Press
2445 River Tree Circle
Sanford, FL 32771
http://www.focusonethics.com

This book was set in Adobe Caslon
Cover Design and Composition by Jonathan Pennell

Library of Congress Catalog Number: Applied For
          Mulling. Emory,
The Mulling Factor: Get Your Life Back by Taking
Control of Your Career:
          ISBN: 0-9708444-7-6

First DC Press Edition
10   9   8   7   6   5   4   3   2
Printed in the United States of America

Disclaimer

I AM A PROFESSIONAL CAREER and outplacement consultant. In that capacity I have had the opportunity to work with thousands of individuals who have lost, are in danger of losing, or are unhappy with their jobs. In this book, examples are drawn from those experiences. I have changed the names, industries, and any other information that was necessary to insure that the individuals involved could not be recognized ... while keeping the elements necessary to retain the validity of these examples. For this reason, any similarity between the situation of an individual that a reader may know and any described in the examples is nothing more than coincidence.

Dedication

THIS BOOK IS DEDICATED to my wife of 25 years, Kathryn, who has taught me how to take control of my life, and to our two children, Allison and Tyler, who remind me of the importance of life balance.

Contents

About
The Author

EMORY MULLING IS CHAIRMAN of The Mulling Companies, an Atlanta-based family of firms handling outplacement, leadership development and retained search. He has been active in career guidance and Human Resources consulting since 1973 and formed his company in 1985. His company is an affiliate of Lincolnshire International.

Mr. Mulling is President of the Association of Career Transition Firms International, North America. He has earned the prestigious certification of Fellow from the Inter-national Board for Career Management and is past president of the Society for Human Resource Management-Atlanta Chapter and the recipient of its "Lifetime Achievement Award."

A former Vice President of Human Resources, Mr. Mulling's background in human resource management includes positions with Fortune 500 companies in manufacturing, food services, distribution, transportation and banking, in both union and non-union environments.

He writes a nationally syndicated column for the American City Business Journals network entitled *People Smarts*, which advises business owners and management on Human Resources issues. He has been featured in numerous national publications including *Time*, *Fortune*, *Kiplinger's*, *Entrepreneur* and *Newsweek*, as well as on radio and television, providing expert advice on career management.

A Georgia native and Vietnam veteran, he has been married for 25 years to his wife, Kathryn, and they have two children, Allison and Tyler.

Foreword

Even Smart People Make The Wrong Choices

THIS IS A BOOK FOR SMART people looking to make the right career choices.

Let's face it, our careers define and shape us; they are the vessels that carry our hopes and dreams. Correctly chosen, they bring us success and well-being. Poorly chosen, they are sinking ships — dead weights that drag us down.

Whether you're fresh out of school looking for your first real job or re-entering the job market after graduate school or fifteen years of raising children, you want this first step to reward you with more than a paycheck.

Or, if you're now suffering the shock of unemployment or the slow torture of being unhappy in your job, the one thing you know for sure is that you want to make the right choice for the next phase of your career. In fact, those who have been "let go" (or "fired," "downsized," "laid off," "forced into early retirement," or "left by mutual agreement") are not so different from those who voluntarily seek a career change. An

*Careers …
poorly chosen …
are sinking ships,
dead weights that
drag us down.*

amazing number of people who have lost their jobs are not looking to replace those jobs but to find a new career altogether.

"I can see that maybe this isn't what I should be doing at all," the career changers say. The recently laid off tell me, "I didn't like that job anyway. Maybe this is a wake-up call … an opportunity to make a fresh start." Both groups are saying the same thing. The only difference is the career changers are taking control and those laid-off are often still in shock.

So the exact circumstance that has propelled you to seek career guidance is not important. What is important is that you've chosen a book to educate yourself about job factors and your own needs before making a choice.

I've been in your position — more than once — and it took me totally by surprise.

Here's my story: I was a precocious teenager. I already had a goal, for my future. I decided when I was fourteen that I wanted to be Vice President of Human Resources for a major company. That was before any of my friends had ever heard of Human Resources, and in fact, before most companies had heard of it.

I became an Eagle Scout and spokesperson for the Boy Scouts of America when I was fourteen. I gave eight speeches in one month including one before the state legislature. I was provided with a press clipping service that same year. As a junior in high school, I was president of student council; as a senior I was president of Hi-Y; and in the yearbook I was named "Most Likely to Succeed." I was on my way to the top.

After college, and a stint in the armed services that included a year in Vietnam, I began working my way up the career ladder in Human Resources. I deliberately worked for a non-union company and then a union company to have experience in both. I switched industries to broaden my knowledge. According to plan, I became Vice President of Human Resources for an industry leader at the age of thirty-two. I was the youngest person with that title in the city of Atlanta.

I'm not telling you this to impress you with my brilliance. I tell you this to impress you with my ignorance ... because, without my having the slightest hint of anything amiss, one fine autumn day I was called into the president's office and fired. I was given no transition time, no severance pay, and no help in finding a new job. They didn't want me to drive my company car home. I had to have one of my employees take me home. I stood on the sidewalk in the shadow of that building where I had worked, holding my personal possessions in a box, waiting for the ride. I was embarrassed to tell my wife what had happened. I was even more embarrassed to tell my in-laws. I was devastated, humiliated, shocked. I was also angry ... and I was scared. I was in shock for three days.

If the emotions of sorrow, anger and fear represented one side of my distress, the other side was doubt. How could they fire me — an aggressive, goal-oriented, hard worker who was full of ideas? What were they thinking? That was an unfathomable mystery to me.

Oh, what wisdom in hindsight! If I had known then what I know now, I would not have been surprised at all. I was a severance waiting to happen. All the signs I now recognize were there in front of me like a billboard, but I couldn't read them.

In a few days I pulled myself together, hired an outplacement consultant, and within seven weeks I had landed a job with one of the companies featured in Peters and Waterman's best-selling book, *In Search of Excellence*. What's more, this company had a cutting edge Human Resources program. I was a regional Human Resources Manager. What could be more perfect?

But I was not happy there. I was frustrated, and I made an early escape. Next, I got a job in Human Resources at a large, old, established bank, but not in the top position. For the next five years, I felt as if I were on vacation. And I'm a man whose idea of a long vacation is five consecutive days! During my last three years at the bank, I was doing some consulting on the side simply to keep myself stimulated, but I'd never considered doing it full time. When a friend — in fact, a woman who reported to me — finally said, "Emory, it's time for you to go," the blood drained from my face. I wasn't ready because this was not what I had planned. But she was right.

I'm still in Human Resources, as you can see, but I've found a job where I thrive. In my eighteen years as a consultant, I have seen over 10,000 people going through job transitions and, not surprisingly, along the way started seeing trends. People were let go, as I was. People were bouncing from job to job, often dissatisfied, as I was. They had, in the past, always thought they would do better next time, but they were beginning to suspect that maybe they wouldn't, that maybe job satisfaction was an impossible dream, and they were scared. I made it my goal to develop a method based on my experience and the experiences of thousands of others to help people make the right career choices.

I've listened to the pain and anger of a thousand downsized, displaced, misplaced Americans. I have put many of them on the path to correct employment. I know that the pursuit of the American dream does not have to be a nightmare of frustration and disappointment.

... the pursuit of the American dream does not have to be a nightmare of frustration and disappointment.

This book identifies a problem — the problem I had, the problem you may have, the problem millions of Americans have — so you can avoid it. And it offers a solution in the form of a tool that has proved successful in guiding thousands of my clients to satisfying, successful employment.

When you have finished this book, I expect you will be among them.

Publisher's Comment

DON'T YOU THINK that virtually every employee, at one time in history, in a given location has had the same dream: working for the "right" boss under the "best" of work environments? In your own life, haven't you dreamed of the perfect job, the perfect working conditions, and an encouraging boss for whom you could work without fear or pressure?

Unfortunately for many American workers — in all types of jobs, at all levels, at all pay scales — the dream job is only that: a dream.

Today, more than ever, people are keenly aware of the importance of working in the "right" environment and for the "right" type of boss. Many of us have worked for the "boss from hell" and can appreciate how important it can be — to our health and emotional well-being — to work under and with a boss with whom you mesh.

For many, however, getting a job — any job — can be the sole priority. And many employees, therefore, find themselves in jobs with little satisfaction or future. Misemployment — a theme that runs through this book — isn't new. People have been misemployed for thousands of years. We're all familiar with people who are great individuals in their own right, but are nestled into jobs for which there is little enjoyment, satisfaction, and personal reward. Perhaps we are those people. Perhaps we've been misemployed. Perhaps we exist in a bad work environment with that "boss from hell." Perhaps, it's just a thought.

What Emory Mulling offers on the pages of this book is something unique: an opportunity to assess yourself, the ability to determine if you are in the "right" work environment, and if you are working with the "right" type of boss. *The Mulling Factor* is a simple tool that assists any interested person in quickly determining if they are misemployed and provides relevant information on how they might change their environment for the better. If you are that person, give *The Mulling Factor* a try. You may be very pleased with the results.

—**Dennis McClellan**
Publisher, DC Press

CHAPTER ONE

Misemployment

- Is the energy and enthusiasm that once defined you bleeding away?

- Does your anxiety level skyrocket as you pull into the company parking lot on Monday mornings?

- Do you emerge from the subway with feet of lead, lugging a briefcase full of unfinished reports you told yourself you would work on at home but didn't?

- Does the happy talk in the elevators drive you to distraction?

- Do you walk around your workplace with your shoulders around your ears waiting for the ax to fall?

- Does the clock move in slow motion?

- Are you spending too much time on tasks that seem unimportant?

- Do you often feel at odds with your boss on important issues?

- Do you want to shout: "How can you people stand this place?!"

If these questions ring a bell with you and your answers are mostly "Yes," you have a problem.

1

- Are your job frustrations spilling over into your personal life?

If these questions ring a bell with you and your answers are mostly "Yes," you have a problem.

The problem is **misemployment**. Misemployment explains why every conversation with close friends inevitably gets around to job frustration or anxiety, why your boss hasn't dropped by your office for a friendly chat in a long time, and why the fast track no longer runs past your office door.

Misemployment affects the happiness and well-being of millions of Americans. It erodes self-confidence and self-esteem. Its impact extends far beyond your work life. Like unemployment, misemployment feeds family problems and contributes to divorce, substance abuse, and depression.

Misemployment is a problem that all too often is ignored until it's too late.

Job surveys suggest the majority of Americans are misemployed. The majority! If that estimate seems extreme, talk to friends and co-workers to find out how many of them are satisfied with their careers. Talk to the recently retired; how many of them feel they spent their working lives watching the clock or calendar? Look at the dour faces of the commuters packed into the bar car as the 5:40 PM train pulls out of Grand Central Station; the men and women

Misemployment is a problem that all too often is ignored until it's too late.

Life is a continuous exercise in creative problem solving.
Michael J. Gelb

2

> Knowing what you can not do is more important than knowing what you can do. **Lucille Ball**

bleakly facing the traffic on the 405 Expressway in Los Angeles.

In over twenty-five years of Human Resources management and career assessment consulting, I have interviewed thousands of individuals and not one has ever challenged the painful assertion that the majority of American workers are dissatisfied with their jobs. Look around you. The majority of your friends, co-workers, bosses or employees are probably misemployed!

Let's be clear. Misemployment is not underemployment. In the nineties this was labeled the "McJob" syndrome and defined as: work, salary and status far beneath one's educational level, skills or ability. Neither is misemployment being in a job that demands a higher skill level than you possess. No, misemployment is more complex and, therefore, more difficult to address.

You may have a prestigious job making a six-figure salary and still be misemployed. You may be a walking definition of success — respected, envied, emulated — and be misemployed. You may be in a mid-level position going nowhere — a classic symptom of misemployment — or right out of college, starting a new career, determined, highly motivated, but heading down the wrong career path. Misemployment affects the 55-year-old partner in a prestigious law firm, the 27-year-old account executive, the 40 year-old

Are you a victim of the "McJob" syndrome?

administrator, and even the occupants of the White House …

Jimmy Carter was misemployed as President of the United States. No wonder the American people voted him out of a job in 1980. Having been forced into a career change, Carter has become perhaps the most successful ex-president in history, a global troubleshooter and peace-maker, best selling author and builder of homes for the poor. Most importantly, Jimmy Carter is a happy, useful and fulfilled man with his abilities appreciated both locally and globally.

Similarly, the keen intelligence, fierce independence and combativeness that served Hillary Clinton so well as an attorney hurt her as the nation's First Lady. She was expected to retreat into the stereotypes she had spent her life resisting: to play up to the cameras, to act like a housewife in the background. As First Lady, she was misemployed. But, fortunately for her, it was a temporary job; and she was able to pursue an opportunity that she felt would realize her full potential. Time will tell, but in her job as senator she may be more appropriately employed because it is a position that allows her to be in the spotlight as an advocate for the causes that incite her passion.

Most of us do not have a term limit on misemployment. We have to draw a line ourselves and say enough is enough.

A pessimist sees the difficulty in every opportunity; an optimist sees the opportunity in every difficulty. **Winston Churchill**

…you are misemployed if you're in the wrong job for your personality.

Where assessment programs are available, they usually assess the wrong things.

To put it simply, you are misemployed if you're in the wrong job for your personality. You know misemployment both by the feel and by the facts.

Stop a moment. Breathe deeply. Drop your shoulders. Let the weight of the world slide off of them. Sit down and let your feet sink into the floor. Relax. You don't have to suffer through years of uninteresting and unrewarding work. You do not have to tolerate a boss with whom you cannot connect. Nor he or she with you! This is not the way it's supposed to be.

Job Satisfaction Is *Your* Responsibility

When you're miserable and misemployed, you can either do nothing or do something.

Doing nothing often appears to be the easiest way to go. Deny, ignore the tell-tale signs of misemployment. Think that any day the situation is going to get better. But if you're truly misemployed, it won't. If you are counting on the company to see your plight and save you, you're grasping at straws. Has your company ever tested you or taken responsibility for making the best use of your talents? Probably not. Eighty per cent of America's workforce is employed by small businesses where assessment tools or career consulting is not usually available. And where assessment programs are available, they usually assess the wrong things.

There is something that is much more scarce, something rarer than ability. It is the ability to recognize ability.
Robert Half

5

Thinking you will be noticed eventually is an invitation to be overlooked or ignored. Leaving your future up to the company is lazy at best — disastrous at worst. When you ignore the inevitable, it blindsides you and catches you unprepared. You kid yourself right up to the minute the ax falls.

Maybe you've already quit trying. Sadly, many individuals have embraced the "salt mine" view of the work environment. They believe that their jobs are supposed to be emotionally unrewarding and unfulfilling; that's the price they must pay for a livelihood. They become lazy or rigid in their thinking. They become creatures of habit, or they believe that change is too complicated or too difficult to effect. They refuse to plan, learn a new skill, re-educate themselves, or take advantage of the opportunities that swirl around them. In many cases, they become the kind of boss or colleague they dislike the most.

Denial of misemployment or giving up on job satisfaction usually has disastrous consequences. The first area affected may result in physical health problems: headaches, unexplained tiredness, back and neck pain, and all the diseases to which stress contributes. (Isn't that all of them?) Mental health is also affected; depression, anxiety and irritability lead the pack as examples in this area. Substance use can become substance abuse.

Sadly, many individuals have embraced the "salt mine" view of the work environment.

Courageous risks are life-giving, they help you grow, make you brave, and better than you think you are.
Joan L. Curcio

Misemployment is often unemployment waiting to happen.

... wouldn't it be better to end your employment on your own terms ...

And if you don't get sick first, the other likely result of doing nothing is YOU WILL BE LET GO. **Misemployment is often unemployment waiting to happen.** Misemployment is often disguised as poor performance. Your dissatisfaction has shown on your face, in your walk, in your productivity. Your termination (past or future) may be part of a general downsizing, but why are you chosen for downsizing instead of the other guy? Could your dislike of the job have anything to do with it? You have been fearing termination for a long time, yet you secretly wish for it. It will end your current source of misery. If you were going to be out of a job, wouldn't it be better to end your employment on your own terms and without the black mark on your record? Of course!

Your only reasonable course is to do something to change your life. But not just anything. A lot of people change jobs when they get sufficiently unhappy but fail to educate themselves correctly on their needs and the characteristics of the jobs they are considering. Thus, they go out of the frying pan into the fire, from one form of misemployment to another. And another and another, as I myself have done.

Now, the first course of action, if you're misemployed or unemployed, is to make a realistic assessment of what you should be doing and where you should be doing it.

> Life belongs to the living, and he who lives must be prepared for changes.
> **Johann Wolfgang von Goethe**

Making an assessment is scary because it may confirm that you are misemployed and point the way to dramatic change. Most change is stressful. But preparation is the best way to manage stress. Preparation overcomes fear: fear of failure, fear of financial disaster, fear of the unknown. As Bear Bryant, the famous University of Alabama football coach, liked to say, "Luck is preparation meeting opportunity." The opportunities are out there. You may have to change your job or elements of your job; but be assured, once you're in the right job, money, advancement and satisfaction will follow.

I know thousands of people who love their jobs. Not every one of them makes a million dollars per year; not every one of them travels the world or controls billion-dollar budgets. But they are happy and satisfied. Most of them have been confused and disappointed at some point in their careers; many were even despondent. Today they are living, breathing, laughing proof that it is possible to be successful and fulfilled.

They arrived there by looking at themselves from a new angle.

> You must be the change you wish to see in the world.
> **Mahatma Ghandi**

> Luck is preparation meeting opportunity.
> **Paul "Bear" Bryant**

CHAPTER TWO

The Right Job

NOW YOU KNOW what misemployment feels like in your gut. It's very different from the feeling of right employment.

You can smell right employment — the excitement, confidence, energy, commitment it engenders — as quickly as you can smell a career soured by fear, disappointment and despair.

You have the right job . . .

… If you get up in the morning thinking, "I can't wait to get to work to try out my new idea" …

… If Sunday night you start to plan what you will do on Monday morning and reach for a pen …

… If you don't want to take a break for lunch…

… If you glance at the clock in the afternoon and say to yourself, "I can't believe it's so late!" …

You can smell … If you laugh a lot …
right employment

9

... If you come home happy ...

... If your boss seeks you out when he/she doesn't have to ...

... If you find yourself telling people you have "a great job" ...

Show Me the Money

But what about the money, you may be thinking. Isn't that supposed to be my goal?

When you were very young, your paycheck may have seemed most important. "How much does it pay?" was the first thing on your mind if not the first thing out of your mouth at a job interview. And when your mother-in-law tells people you "have a great job," she probably means you have a good salary. "Show me the money" may be the driving force for a lot of people, but I say, "Forget the money."

Money shouldn't be the deciding factor of employment. In the first place, job satisfaction is more important than an increment of pay, as you may have learned from being misemployed. Health and happiness are vastly more important than money; misemployment for the sake of money ruins both. If you are misemployed and you find yourself saying, "I can't give up the job because I need the money," you are rationalizing your inaction. The money margin is not worth the unhappiness for forty or fifty hours (or more) — fifty-two weeks a year. But that's not all.

The money margin is not worth the unhappiness

Was **George Allen** correct when he said, "The tougher the job, the greater the reward."

10

Don't chase the money; let the money find you.

The best part about forgetting the money and going for job satisfaction, is that soon the money will find you! Many people who have left lucrative misemployment for less money and more job satisfaction have made that wonderful and unexpected discovery. Their compensation soon equaled or surpassed the compensation they had received when they were misemployed.

If you are satisfied in your job, you will prosper. Happy people get the raises, the promotions, the bonuses, the profits, because they are more productive. That's why I say, "Don't chase the money; let the money find you."

Make yourself indispensable, and you will move up. Act as though you are indispensable, and you will move out.
Jules Ormont

If Not Money, What?

The most meaningful equation I have found for optimal employment is this:

The Right Work
+ **The Right Boss**
+ **The Right Work Environment**

= **The Right Job.**

These three elements are necessary for optimal employment, for a happy productive YOU. These elements are out there. The key question is, will you know them when you see them?

The Work

Of the critical career elements, the one most people recognize as important is the *type of work*, that is, the activity, the profession, the use of particular skills. The work may be number crunching or customer service or desktop publishing. It may be trouble-shooting machines or caring for sick people or teaching. It may be law or dentistry or one of the performing arts.

The choice of work is the part of the equation that concerns us from the moment we graduate from high school and often even before that time. Our choice of work usually determines our further training or college, our college major, and often graduate school. It is for the choice of work that we usually go to guidance counselors, college advisors, placement directors, and career counselors. Sure, we all know people who have chosen the work they do for no reason or poor reasons:

"I'm a teacher because I couldn't decide what I wanted to do … that was, oh, ten years ago."

"I'm supposed to carry on a family tradition."

"I became an administrator because I like working with computers."

And we know people who have chosen a job by stumbling into it. Most often, somebody tells them they know of a job opening, and they apply for it because it is available and they need a job.

… we know people who have chosen a job by stumbling into it.

My job is never work — the only time it seems like work is when I'd rather be doing something else.
Anonymous

12

> Creative minds
> have always
> been known to
> survive any
> kind of bad
> training.
> **Anna Freud**

But by and large, of those who took the trouble to explore their needs and to compare them with the elements that make up employment, most of them focused on the first element: the *work*.

If they were wise, they realized that the choice of work should take into account both aptitude and interest. If they were lucky, they found a consultant who could administer objective tests to assess those two areas.

A Story of Aptitude

A bright young man called Dean came to me, "desperate," he said, to change careers. Before I could say a word, he blurted out his life-long dream: "I've always wanted to be an architect!"

Unfortunately, when I had Dean assessed, using a reliable, finely-tuned diagnostic tool for work aptitude, he scored poorly in his perception of spatial relations. Not a good omen for a budding architect. When I explained this to him, he was disappointed, even downhearted. He insisted the assessment tools had him "all wrong." He saw himself up there with I. M. Pei and Philip Johnson. I said, "If you're feeling lousy right now, imagine spending a fortune trying to get through architectural school and doing poorly. Maybe even worse, imagine how awful you'd feel being a mediocre or marginal architect instead of a marvelous one."

Sales ability can be applied in any field of interest.

13

Another assessment tool showed me Dean did not mind risk-taking. Because of his sales interest and sales ability, he liked the unpredictability of a sales position. I explained that the ability to sell meant he was outgoing, energetic, happy working with loose supervision on his own. Moreover, I explained to him that sales ability can be applied in any field of interest. With some hard work and a modest amount of retooling, Dean landed a sales position selling materials and support services to architects. Today, he's very happy and is a top-producing salesman for his company.

Interest is the other aspect to consider in pursuing work, and you can see how I bore this in mind while guiding Dean toward an area of aptitude.

Sometimes, when aptitude is strong in more than one area, it's easy to ignore interest, as a friend named Leo did.

A Story of Interest

Leo was a dentist I knew, an outgoing, creative fellow living in Chicago. As a young man, Leo got some well-meaning but unfortunate advice: "Financial security is the only career goal." It's a drumbeat many babyboomers have heard. Like many of us, Leo listened to the fears of the older generation. For him, the path to financial security wound through dental school. People will

When aptitude is strong in more than one area, it's easy to ignore interest.

We've entered an era when very good, competent people aren't getting jobs. One remedy is to stand out, to self-promote. If you do, you're going to get the nod over some co-worker.
Jeffrey P. Davidson

14

> Listen to your intuition. It will tell you everything you need to know.
> **Anthony J. D'Angelo**

> Winning isn't everything. Wanting to is.
> **Catfish Hunter**

always have teeth that need attending, he figured. He worked hard, was good at his craft, rising to become Chief of Pediatric Dentistry at a famed children's hospital. He obviously had aptitude for the work.

But Leo was unhappy. In his late thirties, when he could stand it no more, he quit, moved to the South, and never practiced dentistry again.

In college, Leo had enjoyed inventing what might best be called widgets. He had patented a few of them, and they helped pay his tuition. After much soul-searching, he returned to the inventor's bench, designing low cost anti-burglary items, toys, gadgets, and novelty gifts. Today Leo is satisfied, successful and financially secure.

Leo aimed for money — his original mistake — and had the aptitude for dentistry, but ignored his interests. His ultimate career reflected both his aptitude and his interest, and — as a result he prospered financially.

The Wrong Work

When I think of the wrong work, I can't help but think of Meriweather Lewis whose fabulous adventures in the wild unexplored West have been so wonderfully recounted in Stephen E. Ambrose's bestselling book, *Undaunted Courage*. Lewis had left for the uncharted wilderness with men and supplies to follow the rivers and find the mythical Northwest Passage. The exploration took place totally out of reach of his boss and mentor, Thomas Jefferson. Being a self-starter *par excellence*, Lewis led his men for three years through hostile Indian Territory, surviving near-starvation, encounters with wild animals, and calamitous river rapids — with the loss of only one life. He recorded his adventures in a journal and made maps of his journey. Though he struggled with bouts of depression and did without his beloved alcohol for much of the journey, his boundless energy, ingenuity, and leadership were never anything but awesome.

Lewis returned East as a conquering hero, and by previous agreement with Jefferson, settled down in St. Louis to edit his journals and write a book. Not only would the book become a national treasure, but also the royalties from the book and fees for public appearances and lectures were supposed to provide a living for Lewis for the rest of his days. Lewis, distracted by administrative duties — which Jefferson also gave him — perhaps contemplated the journals but never actually finished the work. He apparently felt guilty about his lack of production and failed to answer any of Jefferson's letters of inquiry about the project. He eventually committed suicide without having done any substantial work on the book.

Misemployment. The wrong work and a national tragedy. We can only wish that Jefferson had sent a writer/editor to pick up the

> We made too many wrong mistakes.
> **Yogi Berra**

Many of us have never learned to say "No!" to promotions.

journals, appointed another administrator for the Louisiana Territory, and then sent Lewis out in the wilderness again for another adventure.

The Classic Promotion to Misemployment

I cannot leave the subject of choosing the right work without warning you of the most common mistake managers make by overlooking aptitude and interest. The classic example of doing the wrong work involves a technically competent person who is the best teacher or best technician or best engineer in the department. And what happens? In due time, he or she is made a manager of the department. The promotion is based on the employee's competence and their current work! Their aptitude for or interest in management, which is a separate type of work all its own, is never explored. He or she is almost never assessed for management aptitude or interest, and, even more astounding, the hapless candidate is rarely trained in any management skills.

One of my clients, Ava, represents this unfortunate truth. She is 41 years old, a graduate of a prestigious medical school. For eight years, she worked for a well-known institute. Science was her life. Her idea of job satisfaction was growing viruses in a test-tube. And she was very, very good at it.

Anyone who doesn't make mistakes isn't trying hard enough.
Wess Roberts

17

However, when the institute's director offered her a management position, she took it. Her promotion brought a significant pay increase to $110,000.

Many of us have never learned to say "No!" to promotions. Sometimes we must do just that. If we say "no" to the wrong job, trust me, the right job will come along. In Ava's case, the director was very insistent; he wanted a female in that position.

His needs completely overrode Ava's. Moving into management was a shock neither Ava nor her new staff were prepared to handle. In her view, she was stuck babysitting children who were just a few years out of graduate school. Her interpersonal skills were weak. She became a tyrant.

"This work is sloppy!" she shouted at team members.

"You deserve to be treated like children," she yelled.

Ava needed to be talking to test tubes, not to people.

Eighteen months after she took the new job, after numerous and ineffectual interventions by her boss, Ava was fired. Stunned, she drove home along roads that were empty and unfamiliar at mid-day. She panicked, heading back to her office. She stared at the building in disbelief. Her life was in there.

> If you get up one more time than you fall you will make it through.
> **Chinese Proverb**

"This is all a mistake," she told herself, "a bad dream."

At home, Ava stayed in bed for weeks, refusing to answer the phone. It didn't ring much. When a consultant from The Mulling Companies tried to talk to her about what happened, she insisted, "Those employees got what they deserved. My behavior was totally appropriate. They needed to be whipped into shape."

She clung to this argument for four months. She was bitter, blaming everyone but herself for her problems.

Our assessment showed her as a research technologist, born and trained. Not a manager. Ava is a person with little interest in personal contact. Over time, Ava began to identify her misfortune as misemployment and her optimal job as the one she'd had previously.

Ava is now back in a research laboratory where she thrives. She has authored several important papers, and her work is a major source of grants for her organization.

In the meantime, I hope her former boss has hired in her place a doctor with people skills who is ready to escape the lab, a trained manager with a science background or a biology major with an MBA — in other words, someone who has the aptitude, interest, and skills required for the work called *management*.

Consulting to identify the right work is the bread and butter of many career advisors. At The

Mulling Companies, we do it well; we have the tools. But so do many other consultants. Assessment tools such as the Career Accounts Placement Survey (CAPS)© or the Strong Interest Inventory© are of proven validity and reliability.

Consequently, if you seek guidance from a college placement director or any kind of career consultant, be sure objective instruments such as these are part of your assessment.

Just do what
you do best.
Red Auerbach

The Right Work Is Just the Beginning ...

Remember the equation for optimum employment?

The Right Work
+ **The Right Boss**
+ **The Right Work Environment**

= **The Right Job.**

If it appears that in this book I give the first element short shrift, it's not because I consider the choice of work an unimportant element of optimal employment. Rather, it's because I'm eager to get on to less explored territory.

And, in fact, that territory is far more critical to your happiness on the job than the choice of the right work.

How can I make that statement? I can make it because in my seminars to thousands of people who are questioning their job satisfaction, fewer than five percent wish they were actually doing different work. The two most critical parts of the equation for optimal employment, the ones that account for more than ninety-five percent of job dissatisfaction (or, alas, misemployment), are the boss and the work environment.

Career consulting books generally make only passing reference to the boss and the environment. They aren't generally treated as key elements. And, in the field of career consulting, there are plenty of assessment instruments that point to the right work but, until now, no measure to guide you toward the other two elements: the right boss and the right work environment. Now there is. I call it, rather immodestly, *The Mulling Factor*. **It's the missing piece in the job search puzzle.**

CHAPTER THREE

The Mulling Factor

IF YOU'RE LIKE THE THOUSANDS of individuals we've consulted at The Mulling Companies, you're not leaving a company because of the work itself. In fact, about two-thirds of our clients come to us because of incompatibility with the boss and almost all the rest because of problems with the work environment.

None of them wants to repeat their misemployment.

Finding the right boss and work environment is first a matter of measuring yourself.

But how do you know the right boss and the right work environment? It's not as easy to determine the ideal boss and work environment for your personal work style as it is to determine your interest and aptitude, but, like interest and aptitude, finding the right boss and work environment is first a matter of measuring yourself.

The Mulling Factor

The Mulling Factor is an assessment tool especially designed to identify your work style to help
you clearly understand the kind of boss and work
environment that will allow you to flourish.
Recognizing your own style and requirements
for comfort puts you in charge. *The Mulling
Factor* provides direction for a journey too many
of us undertake without a compass.

    The Mulling Factor incorporates my twenty-
five years of experience in the field and the professional expertise of William P. Brittain, Ph.D.,
an industrial psychologist whose specialties
include program planning, system design, management development, personnel selection, test-
ing and evaluation. Dr. Brittain is a nationally
recognized authority in the application of behavioral evaluation in management and career
development and, like myself, has spent more
than twenty-five years assisting individuals in
finding optimal employment.

    We have agreed there is a strong need for
understanding work style preferences so fewer
career mistakes will be made. Therefore, we have
developed an assessment tool that individuals
could use to make certain that the job they
choose is the best one for them.

    The Mulling Factor assessment has been
administered to a thousand individuals in many
different careers and on all rungs of the corporate ladder. In the five years we've been using

We developed an assessment tool that individuals could use to make certain that the job they chose was the best one for them.

The Mulling Factor in the cases where we have been able to follow up, no one has taken a job that didn't succeed for them. The majority of *The Mulling Factor* graduates have achieved happy, productive employment.

"The things *The Mulling Factor* assessed I had known previously, but never really seriously considered. When they were pointed out to me, it was like: That's it! Of course! You better believe I paid attention to those things when I got the next job. *The Mulling Factor* and its interpretation changed my perspective," said Roger Ellison, a project manager who came to us for consultation. "And I think I have the right job this time. Every day I notice things at work that fit this whole theory. I feel like I have this secret clue no one else has."

For people like Roger, *The Mulling Factor* opens the door to self-discovery. The analysis it provides is critical in helping them select among career opportunities that fit their interest and aptitude profiles. It is not the only tool used in examining fundamental employment concerns; however, it is the compass they use on their voyage through the job market.

The Mulling Factor is composed of statements designed to measure the qualities you believe to be typical of your work style or preferred way of handling work situations. Before you actually look at *The Mulling Factor*, be assured — there are no "right" answers and there is no "right" work style that you should have. Each work style is an asset in the appropriate situation.

This book is based on *The Mulling Factor* and the critical information it gives you. Please take the time to complete *The Mulling Factor* so you will be able to interpret your results as you read the remainder of the book. After reading the following paragraphs, you may begin taking *The Mulling Factor* on page 28.

How to Complete *The Mulling Factor*

The statements or phrases in the assessment instrument are grouped in sets of four. Rate the four statements in each set according to how closely the statement describes you.

- In the circle by the statement that describes you most accurately, write the number 4.

- In the circle by the statement that is the next best description, write the number the 3.

- Your next preference should be marked number 2.

- Beside the choice that sounds the least like you, write the number 1.

An example of a completed set appears before the assessment.

There is no "right" work style that you should have.

In order to get the best results from this assessment, it's important that you respond to each statement in every group and be very realistic with yourself. In some cases, you may feel that all the statements in a group describe your attitudes or feelings. In other cases, it may seem none do. This is typical. Even so, do not use the same number twice in a group — there are no tie scores allowed — and do not skip an item. Remember, there are no right or wrong answers. So, take your time, and consider your responses carefully.

Now you're ready to take the actual *Mulling Factor* assessment, which appears on the following pages.

THE MULLING FACTOR

How to Complete The Mulling Factor

YOUR PREFERENCES should be indicated on a scale of 4 to 1 in each group of phrases. The highest score is 4 and goes beside the statement that represents you **most** accurately. The statement that is the next best description of your preference is assigned the value 3; your next preference should be assigned the value 2. The choice that is **least** appropriate should be assigned the value 1. There should be no duplication of numbers within a group (avoid tie scores).

- For each set of four phrases, enter **4, 3, 2, 1** beside each phrase which describes your preferred work style.

- Use a number **once** beside each phrase

- Remember, there are no wrong answers

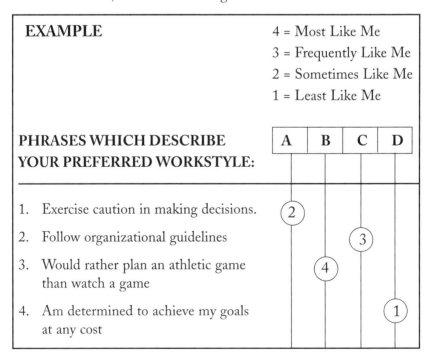

EXAMPLE				
		4 = Most Like Me		
		3 = Frequently Like Me		
		2 = Sometimes Like Me		
		1 = Least Like Me		
PHRASES WHICH DESCRIBE YOUR PREFERRED WORKSTYLE:	A	B	C	D
1. Exercise caution in making decisions.	2			
2. Follow organizational guidelines			3	
3. Would rather plan an athletic game than watch a game		4		
4. Am determined to achieve my goals at any cost				1

THE MULLING FACTOR

Name _____

Date _____

4 = Most Like Me
3 = Frequently Like Me
2 = Sometimes Like Me
1 = Least Like Me

PHRASES WHICH DESCRIBE YOUR PREFERRED WORKSTYLE:

	A	B	C	D

1. Conform and follow company rules

2. At my best when part of a team

3. Self-starter once the goal has been defined

4. Like working for hands-off boss

5. Place a lot of value on loyalty to the organization

6. Don't much like being told what to do or how to do it

7. Most comfortable in stable environments with minimal change

8. Enjoy participating in challenging endeavors

A	B	C	D

Sub-total the values in each column (A,B,C,D)

THE MULLING FACTOR (CONTINUED)

4 = Most Like Me
3 = Frequently Like Me
2 = Sometimes Like Me
1 = Least Like Me

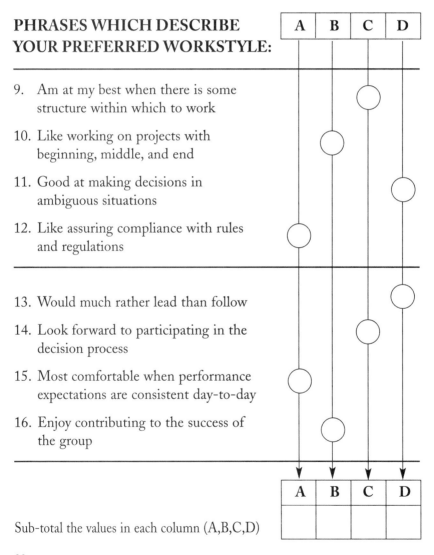

PHRASES WHICH DESCRIBE YOUR PREFERRED WORKSTYLE:

A	B	C	D

9. Am at my best when there is some structure within which to work

10. Like working on projects with beginning, middle, and end

11. Good at making decisions in ambiguous situations

12. Like assuring compliance with rules and regulations

13. Would much rather lead than follow

14. Look forward to participating in the decision process

15. Most comfortable when performance expectations are consistent day-to-day

16. Enjoy contributing to the success of the group

A	B	C	D

Sub-total the values in each column (A,B,C,D)

THE MULLING FACTOR (CONTINUED)

4 = Most Like Me
3 = Frequently Like Me
2 = Sometimes Like Me
1 = Least Like Me

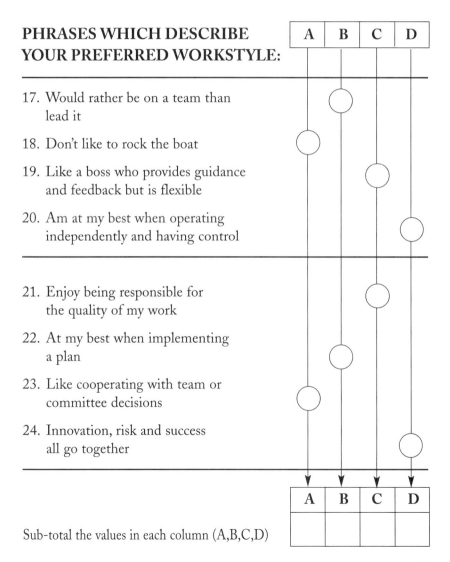

PHRASES WHICH DESCRIBE YOUR PREFERRED WORKSTYLE:	A	B	C	D
17. Would rather be on a team than lead it		○		
18. Don't like to rock the boat	○			
19. Like a boss who provides guidance and feedback but is flexible			○	
20. Am at my best when operating independently and having control				○
21. Enjoy being responsible for the quality of my work			○	
22. At my best when implementing a plan		○		
23. Like cooperating with team or committee decisions	○			
24. Innovation, risk and success all go together				○
	A	B	C	D
Sub-total the values in each column (A,B,C,D)				

THE MULLING FACTOR (CONTINUED)

4 = Most Like Me
3 = Frequently Like Me
2 = Sometimes Like Me
1 = Least Like Me

PHRASES WHICH DESCRIBE YOUR PREFERRED WORKSTYLE:

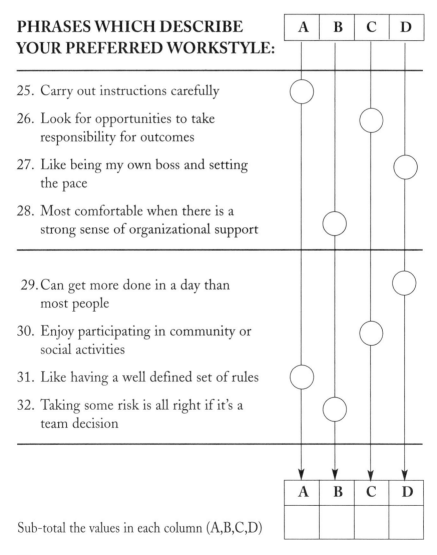

	A	B	C	D

25. Carry out instructions carefully

26. Look for opportunities to take responsibility for outcomes

27. Like being my own boss and setting the pace

28. Most comfortable when there is a strong sense of organizational support

29. Can get more done in a day than most people

30. Enjoy participating in community or social activities

31. Like having a well defined set of rules

32. Taking some risk is all right if it's a team decision

A	B	C	D

Sub-total the values in each column (A,B,C,D)

THE MULLING FACTOR (CONTINUED)

4 = Most Like Me
3 = Frequently Like Me
2 = Sometimes Like Me
1 = Least Like Me

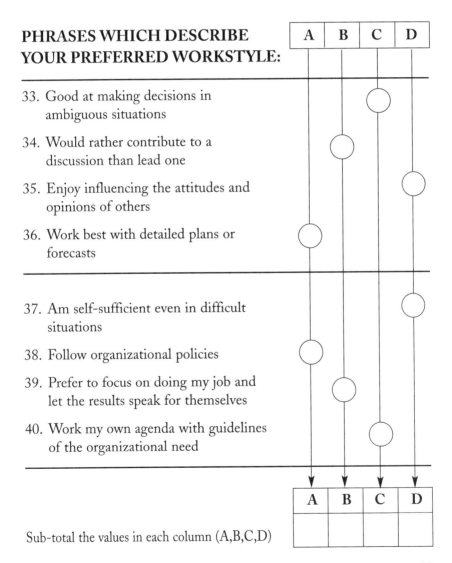

PHRASES WHICH DESCRIBE YOUR PREFERRED WORKSTYLE:

A	B	C	D

33. Good at making decisions in ambiguous situations

34. Would rather contribute to a discussion than lead one

35. Enjoy influencing the attitudes and opinions of others

36. Work best with detailed plans or forecasts

37. Am self-sufficient even in difficult situations

38. Follow organizational policies

39. Prefer to focus on doing my job and let the results speak for themselves

40. Work my own agenda with guidelines of the organizational need

A	B	C	D

Sub-total the values in each column (A,B,C,D)

THE MULLING FACTOR (CONTINUED)

4 = Most Like Me
3 = Frequently Like Me
2 = Sometimes Like Me
1 = Least Like Me

PHRASES WHICH DESCRIBE YOUR PREFERRED WORKSTYLE:

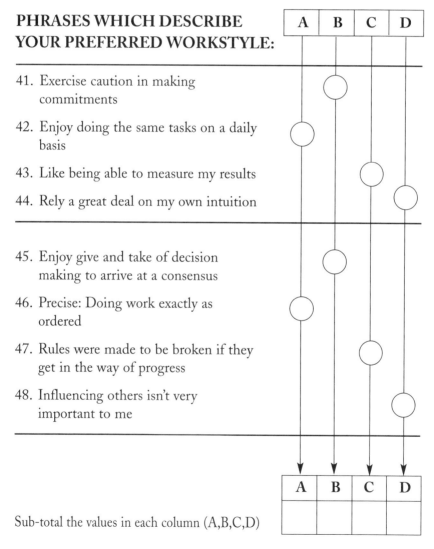

A	B	C	D

41. Exercise caution in making commitments

42. Enjoy doing the same tasks on a daily basis

43. Like being able to measure my results

44. Rely a great deal on my own intuition

45. Enjoy give and take of decision making to arrive at a consensus

46. Precise: Doing work exactly as ordered

47. Rules were made to be broken if they get in the way of progress

48. Influencing others isn't very important to me

A	B	C	D

Sub-total the values in each column (A,B,C,D)

THE MULLING FACTOR (CONTINUED)

4 = Most Like Me
3 = Frequently Like Me
2 = Sometimes Like Me
1 = Least Like Me

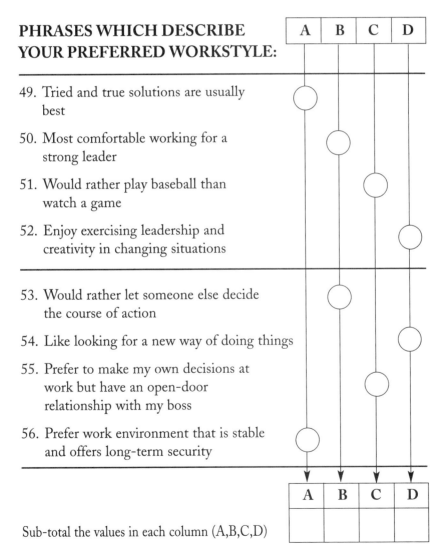

PHRASES WHICH DESCRIBE YOUR PREFERRED WORKSTYLE:

	A	B	C	D

49. Tried and true solutions are usually best

50. Most comfortable working for a strong leader

51. Would rather play baseball than watch a game

52. Enjoy exercising leadership and creativity in changing situations

53. Would rather let someone else decide the course of action

54. Like looking for a new way of doing things

55. Prefer to make my own decisions at work but have an open-door relationship with my boss

56. Prefer work environment that is stable and offers long-term security

A	B	C	D

Sub-total the values in each column (A,B,C,D)

THE MULLING FACTOR (CONTINUED)

4 = Most Like Me
3 = Frequently Like Me
2 = Sometimes Like Me
1 = Least Like Me

PHRASES WHICH DESCRIBE YOUR PREFERRED WORKSTYLE:

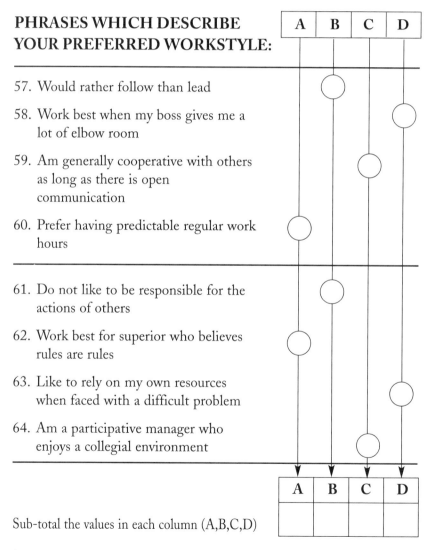

	A	B	C	D

57. Would rather follow than lead

58. Work best when my boss gives me a lot of elbow room

59. Am generally cooperative with others as long as there is open communication

60. Prefer having predictable regular work hours

61. Do not like to be responsible for the actions of others

62. Work best for superior who believes rules are rules

63. Like to rely on my own resources when faced with a difficult problem

64. Am a participative manager who enjoys a collegial environment

A	B	C	D

Sub-total the values in each column (A,B,C,D)

THE MULLING FACTOR (CONTINUED)

4 = Most Like Me
3 = Frequently Like Me
2 = Sometimes Like Me
1 = Least Like Me

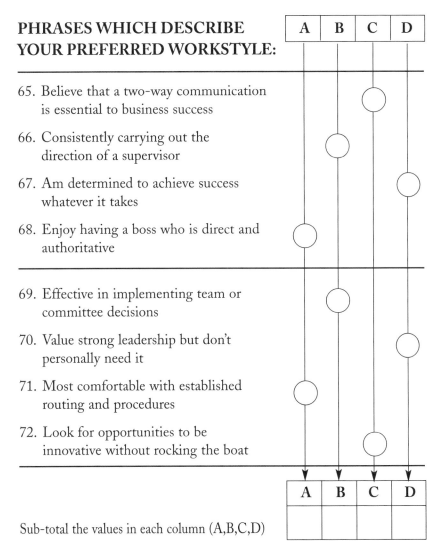

PHRASES WHICH DESCRIBE YOUR PREFERRED WORKSTYLE:

	A	B	C	D

65. Believe that a two-way communication is essential to business success

66. Consistently carrying out the direction of a supervisor

67. Am determined to achieve success whatever it takes

68. Enjoy having a boss who is direct and authoritative

69. Effective in implementing team or committee decisions

70. Value strong leadership but don't personally need it

71. Most comfortable with established routing and procedures

72. Look for opportunities to be innovative without rocking the boat

A	B	C	D

Sub-total the values in each column (A,B,C,D)

THE MULLING FACTOR (CONTINUED)

4 = Most Like Me
3 = Frequently Like Me
2 = Sometimes Like Me
1 = Least Like Me

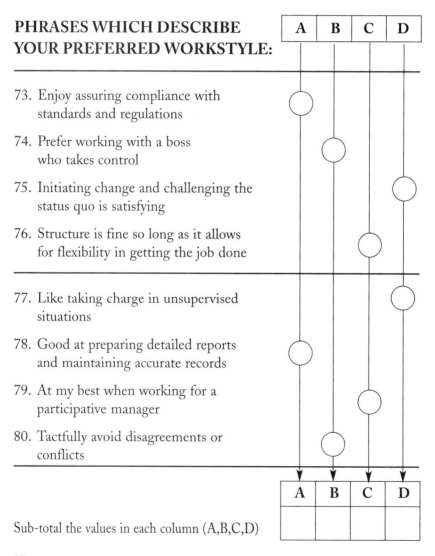

PHRASES WHICH DESCRIBE YOUR PREFERRED WORKSTYLE:

	A	B	C	D

73. Enjoy assuring compliance with standards and regulations

74. Prefer working with a boss who takes control

75. Initiating change and challenging the status quo is satisfying

76. Structure is fine so long as it allows for flexibility in getting the job done

77. Like taking charge in unsupervised situations

78. Good at preparing detailed reports and maintaining accurate records

79. At my best when working for a participative manager

80. Tactfully avoid disagreements or conflicts

A	B	C	D

Sub-total the values in each column (A,B,C,D)

THE MULLING FACTOR (CONTINUED)

Now that you have sub-totaled each page, write the sub-totals from all pages in the spaces provides below to determine your total scores for *The Mulling Factor*

	A	B	C	D
Write Page 29 scores here				
Write Page 30 scores here				
Write Page 31 scores here				
Write Page 32 scores here				
Write Page 33 scores here				
Write Page 34 scores here				
Write Page 35 scores here				
Write Page 36 scores here				
Write Page 37 scores here				
Write Page 38 scores here				

Add the subtotals in each column (A,B,C,D) to determine your total scores for *The Mulling Factor*

A	B	C	D

Your total scores for each of the four columns (A,B,C,D) should equal 200.

Scoring *The Mulling Factor*

Now that you've answered all the questions on *The Mulling Factor* and added up the totals for each column (A, B, C, and D), check to see that the total of the four columns added together are exactly 200. If they're not, you've either made a mistake in addition, failed to rate all the statements, or used the same number more than once in a set.

Now you're ready to interpret your scores. Your scores indicate your preferred "work style"; that is, how you prefer your work environment to be structured and supervised.

If your highest score is under the...

letter A you are a *Conformer*
letter B you are an *Implementer*
letter C you are a *Participator*
letter D you are an *Innovator*

People of all four types are needed in most businesses. All four designations are neutral; each represents an asset in the right situation; each has a downside in the wrong situation.

• Is your highest number clearly higher than all the others? If so, this type represents your preferred work style.

> Ability will never catch up with the demand for it. **Malcolm S. Forbes**

> It is not your aptitude, but your attitude, that determines your altitude. **Zig Ziglar**

- Is your lowest number clearly lower than the others? If so, this type of style is definitely not yours.

- Are the two higher numbers similar and the two lower numbers considerably lower? This pattern suggests you are comfortable with either of the two high-scoring styles.

- Are all your scores evenly distributed? If so, you may find yourself adaptable to a wide range of work styles. More likely, however, you'll have more difficulty finding a niche where you'll flourish; and you may need further consulting.

The Work Style Types and What They Mean

The four style categories are based on a continuum of several related components, some of which you may have recognized as you took the assessment. All together these make up *The Mulling Factor*.

The most comprehensive component is the degree of **autonomy** you require on the job. Your score placed you somewhere on a continuum ranging from needing close supervision (the *Conformer*) to almost total independence (the *Innovator*), with the *Implementer* and the *Participator* scores falling in between.

Another component is **initiative**. If you want to be told when to do what, you scored at the *Conformer* end of the continuum. If you are a self-starter, you scored at the *Innovator* end of the scale.

A third component is **reaction to change**. If you're uncomfortable with shifting winds and new routines, you scored near the *Conformer* end of the scale. If you need change to maintain motivation or keep from being bored, you're closer to the *Innovator* end.

Another component is **risk-taking**. Some, those near the *Conformer* end of the continuum, crave the predictable and safe. Those on the other (*Innovator*) end are exhilarated by the uncertainty of the outcome.

A fifth component is **creativity**, ranging from a preference for following established pro-cedures (the *Conformer*) to a strong preference for generating new procedures, new products, new markets, new methods (the *Innovator*).

The next component on the continuum from *Conformer* to *Innovator* is **loyalty**, an attrib-ute companies want and get most clearly in *Conformers*. Loyalty serves the *Conformer's* need for security. The *Conformer* may feel that fully buying into the company's best interests is the surest way to be valued and treated well in return.

The last component is **confrontiveness**. The *Conformer* does not like to confront or persuade someone of a differing opinion. He may assert himself by holding up the rule book and saying, "You see, here it says …," but he will not fight for one of his own ideas. The *Innovator*, valuing his own ideas above all others, will go to the wall for them, taking on all comers.

The *Implementer* and the *Participator* fall in between these two extremes.

The Mulling Factor puts your reactions to these components together into a work style type, much as the artist for the police department puts together a set of physical features to form a composite portrait someone might recognize. Here are my composite portraits of work style types. Do you recognize yourself? Does your portrait ring true? Most of my clients are amazed at how well their portraits fit them … and they begin to see exactly why they are or have recently been misemployed.

The *Conformer*

Persons who are *Conformers* are orderly, consistent, precise and detailed in their work habits. They prefer to execute clear plans that are well thought out in advance and have clearly established standards and expectations. *Conformers* want a work environment that can be characterized as predictable, stable and guided by clear policy and procedure guidelines. They believe in

rules and structure as the best guidelines to success.

Conformers prefer supportive, clearly defined
relationships; they are quite comfortable yielding
full responsibility to their boss or organization.
They don't want to be in the position of having
to confront strong opposition to sell their ideas
or strategies to others on a regular basis.

Examples of *Conformers*: Clerical/adminis-
trative employees who are satisfied and efficient
in processing paperwork based upon pre-deter-
mined guidelines. Bank tellers are typically
Conformers; so are accountants who are responsible for corporations following the letter of the
tax laws. The engineer who inspects structures to
determine if all technical standards are being met
is a *Conformer*, as is the employee in a manufacturing company who relishes doing repetitive
tasks.

If **The Mulling Factor** ranked you as a
Conformer, the following phrases will sound
friendly and familiar: best when supervised, low
need for individual recognition, controlled, stable, uncomfortable with change, welcomes
defined tasks, resists innovation, strong need for
security, structured, conservative.

Courage is not
the absence of
fear, it is the
conquest of it.
Anonymous

The *Implementer*

If *The Mulling Factor* defined you as an *Implementer*, you tend towards the *Conformer* end of the continuum, but you're most comfortable with somewhat less supervision than a *Conformer;* and you want more autonomy. Your preferred style of work is grounded in cooperation, loyalty and tact. You are steady; you get things done. You are a critical asset in any field of endeavor, an individual who provides invaluable support to colleagues and managers. You're not rigid when it comes to change or innovation. On the other hand, you tend not to lead the charge or seek change. You prefer to implement the innovations of others. *Implementers* go with the flow. You will venture outside well-worn paths and practices, but with some trepidation.

Implementers prefer to work on teams where goals and strategies are discussed openly and calmly and where the team leader or manager is responsible for making decisions and assigning tasks. *Implementers* enjoy working on projects that can be managed efficiently and effectively without unexpected changes or uncertainty. They are good soldiers who enjoy following orders consistently and thoroughly.

Implementers can handle on-the-job disruptions and uncertainty, but only within the context of a unified team approach. They prefer cooperative, supportive relationships in the work environment. They don't want to be in a position of having to lead or to win team support. Interaction is a key word for those *The Mulling Factor* determines to be *Implementers*.

Examples of *Implementers:* Lower to mid-level managers who have the authority to make decisions concerning long-range changes; the brick layer charged with building a wall, given the responsibility to make small variances in the design; or the Information Resources technician working on a team project, relying upon proven technical guidelines, but with the ability to input ideas that might affect the outcome.

If *The Mulling Factor* ranked you as an *Implementer*, the following phrases will seem friendly and familiar: loyal, cautious, little need or desire to be in leadership role, avoids making waves, high need for group achievement, less need for personal achievement, low risk, likes defined goals, and needs support and structure.

> Life belongs to the living, and he who lives must be prepared for changes.
> **Johann Wolfgang von Goethe**

The *Participator*

If *The Mulling Factor* defined you as a *Participator*, your preferred style of work is grounded in cooperation, flexibility, open lines of communication. You like challenges and the freedom to handle them. You like some degree of guidance, but you hate to be bullied or dominated by superiors. You're eager to take responsibility, comfortable working your way through complex tasks. As a *Participator*, you take initiative; you enjoy participating in brainstorming and debates; and you're a great team leader.

You enjoy dealing with ambiguity and uncertainty, so long as broad guidelines are in place and managers are available to provide help, support and constructive criticism. You like risk — but with a safety net. Preferring a give-and-take environment, the *Participator* doesn't mind confronting opposing opinions or selling his or her own ideas forcefully, as long as the debate takes place within an environment of cooperation and congeniality.

Examples of *Participators:* Employee Relations experts who are encouraged in their jobs to interpret and give advice to other employees; loan officers at financial institutions who have the authority and discretion to submit loan applications based upon their expertise and judgment; the team member who modifies a policy manual to better serve a changing marketplace; the leader who is responsible for motivating a group of employees to develop a new product or to service a new market niche; and the police detective encouraged to solve a case using ingenuity and creativity while working within the confines of the law.

If **The Mulling Factor** ranked you as a *Participator*, the following phrases will sound friendly and familiar: minimal supervision, prefers two-way communication, enjoys challenge, self-starter, comfortable and confident with change, as well as, flexible.

The *Innovator*

If your scores from *The Mulling Factor* peg you as an *Innovator*, you're very independent, change-oriented, forceful, and self-sufficient. You're great at convincing others to come around to your side. You'll take a lot of flak without being discouraged or giving up your goal. You're like a Clint Eastwood character or Oprah Winfrey: individualistic, determined, confident in your abilities. You're self-reliant, you like to be in charge of your own agenda, and you prefer working outside the lines. You have high energy and a great need to achieve in new areas.

*Innovator*s need elbow room. On the job and in their personal life, they require freedom to follow their own intuition when meeting challenges or handling unexpected problems. *Innovator*s love risk. They enjoy striking out on their own. They thrive on being independent — of bosses, co-workers, colleagues. They need to be in control; they have little need for direction from above, input from those below, or approval from either. They enjoy pushing their positions, battering the opposition, taking charge. Frequently, *Innovator*s act as agents for change and may even look for opportunities to shake things up.

Examples of *Innovators:* small business own-ers who enjoy Entrepreneurial risks; the dress-designer charged with making a great fashion statement; the athletic coach who has a high degree of freedom and authority to motivate her team, that freedom counterbalanced by the risk of losing each and every game; the financial manager holding high risk portfolios, who has to make quick, independent decisions to grow his clients' accounts. Good sales people are *Innovators* because they are risk takers; each time they get a "no" they can't wait to find out if the next answer will be "yes," while other types hear "no" a few times and they don't want to ask again. *Innovators* are willing to risk start-up money for a new venture. Some make and lose several fortunes without despair because there's always a next time. Some build up a business to success and then get bored with the plateau and take on another new or failing enterprise because they need another risk.

If **The Mulling Factor** ranked you an *Innovator*, the following phrases will sound friendly and familiar: Entrepreneurial, self-reliant, high need for achievement, assertive, impatient, goal-directed, persevering, open to change, independent, innovative, creative, domi-nant, outspoken, driven, open-minded, idealistic.

You may have noticed the ever-present term "team player" was missing from the descriptions above. People often say, "He's a team player" or

"She's not a team player," or they advertise a job opening with the words, "Wanted: Team player." I avoid the term here because it may mean so many things. If by "team player" you mean someone who works for the whole and not just for himself or his own credit, you may be talking about the loyal *Conformer*. If by "team player" you mean someone who brainstorms well in a group, it may be the creative *Participator*. Teamwork can likewise mean being one of several members working separately and independently or, on the other hand, working constantly with give and take between members of the team. Moreover, there may be different roles within each team and you perform one role comfortably and another role with great distress. In a sense, every style can be a team player of one kind or another.

Now that you know how the types are not so much different in kinds as different in degree, you're not bothered by a tie score on *The Mulling Factor* or by scoring high in two categories. You simply fall in between two types. You may have some characteristics that place you more in one type and some that place you more in another, and consequently you may operate somewhat like one type and somewhat like another. I have divided workers —with all of their individual differences — into types in order to create a model I can discuss efficiently. The types are not distinct, absolute, or without exception, but they are valuable to understanding the relationship between job satisfaction and your boss and work environment.

Now that you have scored yourself and learned your style, you are ready to determine the type of boss and work environment you need. In fact, when you read the description of yourself by type, the type of supervision you need was inherent in the description. The next chapter will flesh out these needs. You'll also meet some men and women whose misemployment could have been predicted by *The Mulling Factor*. I expect you'll see something of yourself in their stories.

BUILDING
THE MULLING FACTOR
CHART 1

You: *Conformer*	Your Best Boss:	Your Best Environment:
consistent dependable cautious orderly compliant loyal precise		

You: *Implementer*	Your Best Boss:	Your Best Environment:
helpful organized uncompetitive productive careful committed practical		

BUILDING
THE MULLING FACTOR
CHART 1 (Continued)

You:	Your Best Boss:	Your Best Environment:
Participator		
flexible		
responsive		
assertive		
persuasive		
sharing risk		
communicative		
open to ambiguity		

You:	Your Best Boss:	Your Best Environment:
Innovator		
independent		
risk-taking		
motivated by change		
creative		
self-starting		
confrontive		
convincing		
adventurous		

CHAPTER FOUR

The Right Boss — For You

PHIL WAS A SHY, introverted financial analyst working for a senior vice president in a large entrepreneurial corporation. He believed in keeping his boss informed in detail about every task. In return, he wanted clear directions from his boss every step of the way.

PHIL'S HIGHEST SCORE:			
Conformer			
A	B	C	D
(74)	63	39	24

The boss was his polar opposite. She didn't care about having clearly defined, open lines of communication. She despised details. She took the long view, abdicating short-term management in favor of long-term results. She wanted her employees to be independent leaders.

Phil, increasingly anxious for direction, began scheduling two appointments with his boss every week. He was terrified at the prospect of completing a project only to learn he had gone in the wrong direction. The problem was that most of the time the vice president had no idea what approach to take, she was interested only in results. And she certainly wasn't interested in regular communication with Phil. The more he pursued her, the more she avoided him. The more she avoided him, the more he dogged her until the whole situation became an office joke. That's when he was sent to me.

I soon realized there was nothing wrong with Phil. He was mismatched with his boss. He was a *Conformer*, someone who wants to do the work the way it's supposed to be done. Phil simply had the wrong boss. He needed to find another boss or to manage the one he had to assure that his needs for reassurance and strong direction were met.

The right boss, you may recall, is one of the key elements of the equation:

The Right Work
+ **The Right Boss**
+ **The Right Work Environment**

= **The Right Job.**

For most people, the boss is the most important element, illustrated by the fact that because

For most people, the boss is the most important element, illustrated by the fact that having the wrong boss accounts for about two thirds of misemployment.

> All change is
> not growth; all
> movement is
> not forward.
> **Ellen Glasgow**

having the wrong boss accounts for about two thirds of misemployment.

If you have the wrong boss, how do you know it?

"Easy," you may say, "he's a jerk."

More likely, he's not a jerk; he's just not a good match for you, and you're both frustrated over your misemployment (or his). Determining the kind of boss you need is easy now that you've taken *The Mulling Factor*.

You've identified your work style preference. You are either a *Conformer*, an *Implementer*, a *Participator*, or an *Innovator*. Now you're ready to put that information to work matching the person you are with the kind of boss for whom you are best suited.

Conformers and the Right Boss — the *Controller*

If, like Phil, you're a *Conformer*, you'll prefer to work for somebody who exercises authority in a calm and organized manner with a minimum of debate and confrontation. Someone who insists on going by the book and is clear about his expectations. Someone who puts a high value on employee loyalty. You want a boss who'll accept your input but won't expect you to sell or debate your ideas. I call this kind of boss a *Controller*.

> *Words like "creativity," "independence" or "initiative" are scary notions to the true **Controller**.*

The *Controller* boss operates strictly his or her way and doesn't look to subordinates for input, advice or assistance. The *Controller* boss requires that all decisions, all initiatives, all ideas must flow from him or through him. Sure, you'll hear this boss say words like "creativity," "independence" or "initiative" when discussing traits he or she values in an employee, but in reality these are scary notions to the true *Controller*. Exercising your own personal style and approach is incompatible with working for the *Controller* boss. The *Conformer* works well with this boss because he or she is comfortable with a tight management style.

You're likely to find an effective *Controller* boss in a highly regulated industry such as utilities, a manufacturing plant with tight controls, an engineering project where there cannot be any mistakes, or the military services.

*Conformer*s are least comfortable with supervisors who expect them to act as sounding boards while the supervisor clarifies his or her own thinking by constantly debating or discarding options. If you're a *Conformer*, you're not comfortable with ambiguity or loose delegation of authority.

Creativity is allowing yourself to make mistakes. Art is knowing which ones to keep.
Scott Adams

Things do not change; we change.
Henry David Thoreau

A *Conformer* with the Wrong Boss — a Cautionary Tale

Phil, whose story opened the chapter, was an example of a misemployed *Conformer*. Gregory is another.

GREGORY'S HIGHEST SCORE:			
Conformer			
A	B	C	D
(68)	56	40	36

Gregory worked for a medium-sized firm of CPAs. He was very structured in his work, and his specialty in tax accounting suited him well. He could analyze the new tax laws and apply them, but the changes in those laws were about as much change as he could handle. He didn't like organizational change imposed on him. New office procedures or expectations bothered him; and, if he had to adjust to something new, he wanted full instructions. He wanted just to "do" taxes, not to develop new ways to do taxes.

Two partners owned 80% of Gregory's company. They seemed to want self-starters and team players. If they gave their employees an idea, they wanted them to run with it. Gregory didn't like to run with anything. He was misemployed.

How long could the company afford to keep someone the company itself avoided?

While the mismatch of Gregory, the *Conformer*, and his bosses was not as great as the mismatch between Phil and his boss, Gregory's mismatch put him under great stress. As a result, he turned caustic to his staff and his peers. He would say, "Do it THIS way," meaning HIS way, and "You'd have to be stupid to do that!" He even said inappropriate and hostile things to people at company social gatherings. Frankly, by the time he was sent to me for executive coaching, his co-workers hated his guts.

Meanwhile, Gregory's bosses had adapted to the situation, sending him fewer and fewer things to do because they were afraid of his temper. How long could the company afford to keep someone they avoided?

I executive coached Gregory on his communication style and offered him alternatives to the "shut up and listen" school of management. But the most useful thing I showed him was that his hostility was a result of being misemployed. Gregory was not a bad person; he didn't want to treat his colleagues badly. He was simply stressed by having the wrong kind of supervision. Once he understood that his mismatch with his bosses was the source of his frustration, and not the ineptitude of his staff and peers, he was able to treat them better. Understanding the problem goes a long way towards correcting it.

During the time that I was coaching him, Gregory confided to me that he was in a bad marriage — it seemed that his tendencies as a *Conformer* did not go well with his wife's

Coaches: motivate, discipline, teach, and reward.

freewheeling style either. The more he was stressed at home, the more he needed to be a *Conformer* at work to feel in control.

Ideally, Gregory would have worked at a different job, but his eventual realization of style differences enabled him to manage his situation and he stayed where he was. His subordinates stopped running to his boss while his boss started giving him the tax work that he was capable of doing.

Implementers and the Right Boss — the *Coach*

Implementers are comfortable with supervisors who will seek out ideas and input from them, who are flexible in their approach to problems, but, at the same time, reserve responsibility to make decisions and to intervene at any time. *Implementers* want to make their ideas count, but they don't like to push too hard or be constantly forced into decision-making roles. *Implementers* work best for what I call the *Coach* boss.

The *Coach* decides on the strategy, the game plan, and gives the team frequent guidance and support as they implement it. Athletic coaches, as the name implies, are usually *Coach* types. They are hands-on managers and physically close by. They are there during the games. They may send in the plays — or they may not — if you're good at calling your own. They motivate, discipline, teach, and reward. They let you have individual glory for your deeds, but they take credit for the overall results.

I think of the hugely successful athletic coaches like Bear Bryant of the University of Alabama, Tom Landry of the Dallas Cowboys, or Lenny Wilkens of the Atlanta Hawks. But great coaches exist in any field. The junior high school teacher who took you under her wing and set you on the right path was probably a *Coach* boss of her class. The chief loan officer at the bank might be a *Coach* to the loan officers, encouraging them to bring in loans without violating the guidelines. He would let them be a little creative but within clear limits, and he was always ready to jump in when there was a problem. In similar ways, the manager of customer service might be a *Coach* boss to the customer service representatives. I also can think of a really effective *Coach* boss who is the CEO of the holding company for a major utility — a regulated industry with strict guidelines.

Implementers with the Wrong Boss — Two Cautionary Tales

Karen was an *Implementer*, but she didn't know it when this story began. She had been happily working in sales in the Midwest but she wanted, for personal reasons, to move East where she had family connections. So she uprooted her family

KAREN'S HIGHEST SCORE:			
Implementer			
A	**B**	**C**	**D**
53	(69)	51	27

and made the move. She was looking for a sales job and immediately sought out an old family friend, "Uncle" Edwin, who had a company in the same industry. He was delighted to see her, and she was relaxed and confident with him. She presented herself well, and Edwin hired her without giving her the usual scrutiny. He didn't even call Karen's previous boss to talk about her work.

It turned out that this family friend needed an *Innovator* as an employee, someone who could make cold calls and win new business. This wasn't Karen. Among other things, she had a fear of rejection. She hadn't recognized this fear because she hadn't been going out and getting new business in her old job. She had actually coordinated old business and grown existing accounts. Though she had thought of herself as selling, she was mostly just taking orders. There's a big difference. Karen was unable to do what she had to do for Edwin and was too proud to ask the other sales associates for help.

Therefore, I was not surprised to learn she had made only a few sales in the first two or three months on that job. She could have followed up on prospects after the initial contacts had been made or developed sales in established accounts. But her boss didn't know her strengths or what kind of direction and support she needed. When Edwin did put pressure on her for results, she grew defensive and difficult. He soon had to let her go, an especially embarrassing outcome because of the close family connection.

The sad thing was Karen went to work immediately in the same situation — different product but the same market with the same degree of autonomy and, of course, the same result. She lasted four months. She didn't realize she didn't have the sales temperament. Today she's in an administrative role with a supportive boss, a *Coach*, right down the hall. With her nice personality, great self-presentation and efficiency, my guess is she's right for the job and happy at last.

While Karen had struggled under too little supervision, Ralph, also an *Implementer*, was too rigidly supervised. A chemist with a master's degree, Ralph headed up a lab for a pharmaceutical company. He was having trouble satisfying his Ph.D. boss. The boss wanted Ralph to keep

RALPH'S HIGHEST SCORE:			
Implementer			
A	B	C	D
50	(66)	49	35

a tighter rein on the laboratory staff and show him more evidence of step-by-step procedures. The stringency the boss wanted didn't seem necessary to Ralph, but each day he resolved to supervise the techs more closely. He usually went home without having made any progress. It was the boss who sent Ralph to me for executive coaching.

We soon established that Ralph was an *Implementer* and the boss was a *Controller*. They were not mismatched far enough for Ralph to see the problem clearly. But once he did, it became a matter of satisfying his boss' need to control while not bearing down too hard on the lab techs, who were perfectly capable of doing their research without every step being monitored. Together we found some ways for Ralph to better manage the boss and his staff. Satisfying supervisors who are not quite your type is an art I'll discuss fully in Chapter Six.

Participators and the Right Boss — the *Delegator*

If your scores suggest you're a *Participator*, you need flexibility. You prefer supervisors who provide broad guidelines instead of rigid rules. You want a boss who is available and interested in your work and who values and evaluates your point of view, rather than one who acts

> When you have a dream you've got to grab it and never let go.
> **Carol Burnett**

unilaterally. The boss who best meets the Participator's needs is the Delegator.

The Delegator boss sets the goal, may suggest the appropriate process of approach, and then turns it over to you. She allows you a lot of independence but wants to be periodically informed about your progress.

Working for a Delegator is a good match if you're independent enough to take some initiative, but not so independent that you cut the boss out of the loop. You don't have to ask permission for everything, but you do have to be prepared to explain what you've done.

Some of the greatest CEOs of the biggest companies have been Delegators; for example, Roberto Goizueta, the late Chairman and CEO of The Coca-Cola Company, was a Delegator. A CEO doesn't have time to manage as closely as a Controller or Coach, but he has to keep tabs on some things because so much is at stake. In the retail industry, for example, Delegator bosses make good head buyers, giving a lot of freedom to the buyers to exercise their sense of style but being available and wanting to be kept abreast of such things as totals spent relative to budget.

If you're a Participator, avoid autocratic and controlling superiors at all costs. You'll be miserable with a strong-willed, "dominant" boss who refuses to consider other points of view or perspectives. At the same time, you won't be happy with disengaged managers who are totally

The boss who best meets the **Participator's** *needs is the* **Delegator.**

If you can dream it, you can do it.
Walt Disney

results-oriented or with bosses who don't take part in or promote team interaction. You don't mind being held accountable — after all, you have confidence in your ideas and abilities. But you don't want to feel that you're out there all alone.

Participators and the Wrong Boss — More Cautionary Tales

Kathy was a *Participator* in the information resources industry. She was a team leader and created a good "feel" in her department of technically competent people.

They did good work. Recently, her team initiated a consumer survey, and she thought everything was going fine. That is, until her boss, Tim, casually asked a team member in the hallway how things were going. "Great," the team member replied and proceeded to elaborate on their new initiative. This was the first the boss had heard about the project. He was furious and, in a knee-jerk reaction, sent a nasty e-mail to Kathy.

Kathy in turn was hurt and bewildered. She had no idea he needed to know every project her team undertook. Wasn't she the leader? Didn't he think they were responsible enough to do it on their own? She was angry that he thought she needed someone looking over her shoulder. Her

KATHY'S HIGHEST SCORE:			
Participator			
A	B	C	D
29	42	(68)	61

team would get the results, and that should be enough.

But Kathy's boss was a *Coach*; he needed to be involved. They simply were not a good match.

Participators, being one of the two middle categories of work style, can also be mismatched by having too little direction. Sherman is a case in point.

Sherman was an architect and a manager of an architectural team. As a manager, he didn't know how to delegate well. Because of this, he was sent to me for executive coaching. I taught him the skills involved in delegating. But in the process I saw how little help Sherman's boss, Bill, gave him. Bill, in addition to being his boss, was the firm's owner and founder and had been a manager for IBM for twenty-five years. He was either unwilling or unable to teach, but being no

SHERMAN'S HIGHEST SCORE:			
Participator			
A	B	C	D
36	52	(63)	49

Innovators flourish when given free rein.

dummy, recognized Sherman's needs — and gave the teaching job to me. By being a surrogate for the guiding kind of boss Sherman needed, I could help make Bill successful in this instance, even as an *Abdicator* boss.

Innovators and the Right Boss — The *Abdicator*

Innovators work best either where they have no direct boss or where the boss is totally results-oriented. (For example, they are willing to concede absolute control over day-to-day strategies and operations as long as high-level goals and targets are met.) *Innovators* flourish when given free rein. The *Abdicator* makes an ideal boss.

The *Abdicator* is the complete opposite of the *Controller* boss. He takes a total hands-off approach to management. He says, "Here's the goal, here are the resources, now get to it." He doesn't have to know how you did it because all he cares about are the results. He'll also be happy for you to get credit for your work because he knows he'll get credit for having chosen you. The *Abdicator* boss often has "star quality" and gets "glory" from clients or the public. The employee who works for the *Abdicator* must be willing or eager to take full initiative in meeting deadlines, establishing guidelines, determining strategies and tactics.

Sales managers need to be *Abdicator* bosses because salesmen typically are self-starters. Anyone who manages people in creative industries such as interior design or advertising had better be an *Abdicator* because control often inhibits creativity.

If you're an *Innovator*, you should avoid autocratic, authoritarian or controlling superiors. *Innovators* can tolerate forceful supervisors but only if the supervisor listens well and is receptive to strong challenges from below. Micromanaging is intolerable. As an *Innovator*, you'll be misemployed to some extent with any boss who wields more control than the *Abdicator* boss will. Your nightmare boss is someone who wields military chain-of-command-type authority, allowing no give and take, no sharing of information with colleagues, where everyone but the supervisor herself is out of the loop.

Innovators with the Wrong Boss — Still More Cautionary Tales

Mike was an *Innovator*. Based on his experience in other start-up situations, he was hired as

MIKE'S HIGHEST SCORE:			
Innovator			
A	B	C	D
30	41	58	(71)

Ability is of little account without opportunity.
Napoleon Bonaparte

CEO of the start-up subsidiary of a large company. Thinking it was his mission as CEO, Mike then hired his top management without consulting his superior. Also, Mike had millions of dollars at his disposal and he put them to work. He proceeded to make a lot of aggressive moves to get the start-up company moving as fast as possible.

Mike reported to the chief financial officer of the parent company. He was an alum of a Fortune 100 company and was fiscally conservative and systems-oriented. This CFO was uncomfortable about the start-up; it was the first this company had ever done. And, to nobody's surprise but Mike's, he was a *Coach* boss.

The CFO wanted to be kept informed of everything in order to be able to keep his own boss informed. Mike, on the other hand told his new reports, "I have a lot of confidence in you. So let's get it done." He didn't tell them how to do it. That was his own management style, and he assumed his supervisor's as well.

The CFO had several little talks with Mike. "Slow down, don't take so much risk," he'd say. Mike didn't hear. The boss also asked a lot of questions. That was a clue that his boss wanted to be kept informed, but Mike didn't catch on. A CEO has autonomy is all Mike knew. Mike was fired "out of the clear blue." It was clear all right.

Later I'll talk about what Mike could have done if he'd really heard and understood what his

> We cannot become what we need to be by remaining what we are.
>
> **Max Du Pree**

boss was saying. But *Innovators* are not usually the best listeners, and "course correction" is not usually in the *Innovator's* vocabulary.

After I consulted with Mike in our career transition process, he considered a job offer from a holding company that had been through start-ups before and may have been more comfortable with giving responsibility to an *Innovator* like himself. Mike knows now that he must find out what kind of a boss will supervise his efforts, and I've given him pointers on how to do that. With this information, Mike has every likelihood of making a right match and succeeding at his next job.

Ron was another *Innovator* too closely controlled. He'd been given the job of spearheading a new product line in the Pacific Rim, and he was going great guns. Among other tactics, he offered a whole array of discounts for high volume orders. Ron knew discounting was inconsistent with the company's pricing strategy, but he wanted to get the ball rolling fast to discourage new competitors from jumping into the market.

RON'S HIGHEST SCORE:			
Innovator			
A	**B**	**C**	**D**
25	45	52	(78)

He'd make up the difference "some other way," and he did. Once he'd captured the market, who cared about the pricing? Everyone at the home office was talking enthusiastically about the success of the roll-out. Everyone, that is, except Ron's boss, John.

John saw that Ron had exceeded expectations by every measure, but John also noted that the effort had not been conducted the way he himself would have done it and, worse, without asking for his input. John was a *Delegator* boss, not an *Abdicator*. The mismatch between John's supervisory needs and Ron's need to be independent was the cause of discontent; jealousy played a part as it often does when *Innovators* succeed on the watch of a boss other than an *Abdicator*. John fired Ron in spite of Ron's success; he was high enough in the company to do that with impunity. That's the way the big boys play. It was called a "personality clash," but I call it a mismatch.

Ron came to me in outrage. Once he understood his scores on **The Mulling Factor**, he was less bitter. He prudently decided to go practice his profession where no one could tell him what to do. He now has his own company and is a successful marketing consultant.

> The only disability in life is a bad attitude.
> **Scott Hamilton**

The Stressed or "Bad" Boss

In recounting these stories of bosses and employees, I haven't described the boss or the employee as a bad person or an inferior type; they were only mismatched. You may still insist, "No, my boss was really a jerk."

I don't know your boss. But I do know that very, very few people set out to be jerks. Almost no one says to himself, "I'm going to use these people for my own gain, mistreat them, then fire them when they get in my way or I'm finished with them." Just as Phil, the misemployed *Conformer*, acted badly under the stress of that situation, bosses can also react badly under stress. Anyone can appear to be a jerk when they are acting under situations that cause them to be severely stressed.

So next time, do yourself and your future boss a favor: use *The Mulling Factor* and find the right boss for you. Believe me, you'll both appreciate it!

BUILDING
THE MULLING FACTOR
CHART 2

You: *Conformer*	Your Best Boss: *Controller*	Your Best Environment:
consistent	hands on	
dependable	looks over shoulder	
cautious	checks work	
orderly	monitors set procedures	
compliant	expects no input from you	
loyal	firm	
precise	fair	

You: *Implementer*	Your Best Boss: *Coach*	Your Best Environment:
helpful	teaches	
organized	directs	
uncompetitive	steps in often	
productive	listens to you	
careful	motivates	
committed	sets goals	
practical	assigns roles	
	establishes procedures	
	supports you	

BUILDING
THE MULLING FACTOR
CHART 2 (Continued)

You: *Participator*	Your Best Boss: *Delegator*	Your Best Environment:
flexible	sets over-all goals	
responsive	leaves methods to you	
assertive	steps in when you ask	
persuasive	requires infrequent reports	
sharing risk	advises	
communicative	challenges you	
open to ambiguity	receptive to your ideas	
	encourages self-development	

You: *Innovator*	Your Best Boss: *Abdicator*	Your Best Environment:
independent	rarely present	
risk-taking	strategic thinker	
motivated by change	hands-off	
creative	trusts you to do the job	
self-starting	empowering	
confrontive	focuses on results	
convincing	decides quickly	
adventurous	expects self-development	

CHAPTER FIVE

The Right Work Environment— For You

*Because you're
successful in
one work
environment
doesn't mean
that you'll be
successful in
another.*

B RAD WAS MAKING $140,000 a year as head of market research for a California company that manufactured products for the medical industry.

The work environment was loose, even by southern California standards. On the days he showed up at the office, Brad wore jeans and moccasins; socks were for special occasions. On Fridays, he, his boss, and a group of women from the office liked to head to a restaurant for margaritas and tequila shooters. Truth was, work was a lot of fun. His boss didn't care what he wore or said or did as long as he caught the market drift.

BRAD'S HIGHEST SCORE:			
Participator			
A	**B**	**C**	**D**
35	39	(68)	58

Brad had an uncanny ability to predict the styles that were going to be popular … what markets were available … what to avoid. His marketing skills were so great he was offered a big position with a competitor on the other side of the country. He accepted. That, as it turned out, was Brad's big mistake.

When he moved his family from California to a city in the South, things were very different. At the office, men and women dressed conservatively. A sports coat was considered radical; suits were de rigueur, even in the sweltering summer. As had always been his practice, Brad wandered in and out of people's offices as if he were taking a walk in the park. He thought he was simply being friendly. He hardly noticed that, unlike his California company, these office doors were often closed.

Brad even had a physical style that was out of sync with his new environment. "He takes up too much space," one of his colleagues said. It was true. He walked fast, he had a gait that attracted attention, he gestured expansively. "Weird" was the word out on Brad. Total environment mismatch.

Next thing, Brad's boss challenged his market analyses. Then Brad got reprimanded for inappropriate behavior, then written up for poor performance. "What's up around here?" he wondered. "I can't figure this place out." Even though Brad had damaged himself almost beyond hope,

> Life isn't about finding yourself. Life is about creating yourself. **George Bernard Shaw**

he was sent to me for executive coaching to see if he could change.

I helped him understand the error he was making: his inability to mesh with or even comprehend his work environment. So accustomed was he to his California environment where he could do his own thing that he failed to adapt to his new one. I even gave him lessons in walking with dignity, keeping his voice softer, and his hand gestures smaller, though it seemed a shame to rope a flamboyant man in so tight.

Brad tried hard to change. He'd bought a new house and put his kids in private schools. But it was too late. His on-the-job credibility was too far gone. The next thing he knew, he was out the door and into our firm's outplacement program. Brad learned a hard lesson: because you're successful in one work environment doesn't mean that you'll be successful in another. Knowing the work environment that will nurture you is critical in any job search.

Once Brad understood what work environment was best for him, he was able to find another top position back in California near his family. I picture him now with a cell phone and a lap top crunching the numbers through sunglasses on Malibu Beach.

The work environment, sometimes called company culture, is, along with the work and the boss, the last of our three elements that define the right employment. I'm not just talking about official corporate protocol, but the "feel" of the place, what is accepted and what is not, what is encouraged or discouraged in terms of an individual's "work style." The work environment includes how decisions are made, how the work is structured and how communication occurs, whether directly, one-on-one; by memo or e-mail; behind closed doors; or open meetings. Environment involves the way people relate to each other, that is, the social style, and sometimes the physical structures which promote that style of relating, for example, long halls with closed doors or open clusters of work stations.

Let's be clear, none of the work environments identified in this book are, by definition, wrong, and no one environment is intrinsically better than another. Each can be viable and supportive; each fits the needs of certain types of individuals. Some investment firms, for example, work on the principle of risk avoidance. A person well-matched for work in such a firm will be less successful in an aggressive, sales-driven environment. *The Mulling Factor* has identified the work environment that will be the most comfortable fit for you, for your personal as well as your career needs. Without a compass such as *The Mulling Factor*, regardless of how talented and hard-working you are, you may still make career mistakes that lead you to years of disappointment and frustration.

No one environment is intrinsically better than another.

The sanctity of the pecking order does not encourage stars except at the top.

Conformers and the Right Work Environment

Conformers work best in jobs with clearly defined responsibilities built around recognized practices. They are dependable in following procedures. *Conformers* prefer things to be fixed and predictable, right down to starting and quitting times. They do best when their job and responsibilities are clearly defined and closely directed. They want their objectives, strategies, and tactics dictated from above. They are not comfortable being asked to make changes or adjustments. *Conformers* work best in what I call a *Bureaucratic* environment.

A *Bureaucratic* work environment limits employees' responsibility. It has written procedures that control, direct and guide workers as well as managers. It is organized around a chain of command. Power and responsibilities are delegated in structured, rigid order. The sanctity of the pecking order does not encourage stars except at the top. And, since information is power, information is not given out freely but only on a need-to-know basis.

Signs of a *Bureaucratic* environment are lengthy procedure lists; endless forms to fill out to get change in work procedures, purchasing or vendors; and time clocks and sign-in sheets and schedules for coffee breaks. Another clue might be hierarchical parking: the higher executives have covered parking near the building while the lower-level employees may have to fend for themselves in a distant lot. *Bureaucratic* environments often have long halls lined with offices with closed doors and titles on them. You have to make an appointment to see your superiors.

The *Bureaucratic* work environment preferred by *Conformers* can typically be found in large companies with a long history of accomplishment. Federal, state, and large governments offer *Bureaucratic* environments, as do the military services. The airlines also have a *Bureaucratic* environment as they are highly regulated, with detailed schedules ruling activity, and exacting safety controls. Few people in an airline can "fly by the seat of his pants" today. Also, hospitals and health care centers are usually *Bureaucratic* because of safety and liability concerns. Some delivery companies, mail order companies, many school systems, nursing homes, the upper levels of church hierarchies, and monastic orders all tend to be bureaucracies.

Royalty exemplifies the *Bureaucratic* environment where the established rules are centuries, not merely decades, old. Rigid hierarchy and much protocol determine accepted behavior; hats and coats must match; and the monarch's birthday is celebrated on a traditional day regardless of his or her actual date of birth.

Anyone who upstages the monarch is squelched and mavericks must abdicate.

Conformers are least comfortable in small entrepreneurial companies or start-up situations in larger organizations, where people seem to be "winging it." Conformers prefer to come into situations that are functioning smoothly. Conformers do poorly in situations where the "wheel is being reinvented," dramatic restructuring is underway, or change is constant.

Conformers in the Wrong Work Environment — Cautionary Tales

Ted was a middle manager in employee relations in the Human Resources Department of a manufacturing company. He worked at corporate headquarters. He knew the regulations coming and going. He had caught a number of slips and probably saved the company from untold trouble. The business climate in his industry may have been changing and required some innovation to remain competitive, but that was for his superiors to handle. He could be the reliable custodian of the rules and regulations. He could enforce the policies. "Ask Ted," was a familiar

Conformers do poorly in situations where the "wheel is being reinvented," dramatic restructuring is underway, or change is constant.

TED'S HIGHEST SCORE:			
Conformor			
A	B	C	D
(71)	60	42	27

line before a questionable action was taken, and Ted knew the answers by heart.

Then the company was sold and Ted accepted a transfer to a large satellite operation. Out in the field, the environment was freewheeling. The new president was a renegade who didn't know how to spell R-U-L-E-S. Folks would come and tell Ted what they wanted to do and ask him to figure out a way they could do it. They didn't want him to cite the relevant regulation but to juggle the rules and find loopholes to accommodate what they needed. They wanted exemptions and special cases. Ted wanted only to protect the company from discrimination cases and to enforce consistency. The management didn't want to hear what Ted was saying. He was a barrier to business now — not a keeper. The struggle got personal, and he was fired.

Ted came to me in outplacement. He put into focus what he had learned about business environments the hard way. Most importantly, he learned how to assess environments from the outside. He researched prospective employers and got a better-paying job in a more structured environment where they appreciated his impeccable record in company protection.

Ava, the research physician you met in Chapter Two, was another *Conformer* who was moved from a *Bureaucratic* environment, where she thrived, to a *Democratic* environment where she became the "manager from hell." In the lab,

> There's an important difference between giving up and letting go.
> **Jessica Hatchigan**

she was immersed in procedures and highly detailed, hierarchical tasks to be accomplished in a certain order. Her test tubes performed in a predictable fashion. She wrote up her results in papers which, after a standard peer review process, would be published, and in turn, would stimulate grants for more research.

When Ava was chosen to manage the whole department, not only was she taken from the work in which she had succeeded (medical research) and given work for which she was ill-suited and untrained (managing), but she was also moved into a *Democratic* environment completely foreign to her. The department included not only a research lab, but also a marketing and public education unit. Her job now included communicating with and managing bright people with a variety of skills, minds of their own, and lives outside of their careers. Ava was mismatched not only with the work but also with the environment, a double whammy that spelled doom.

AVA'S HIGHEST SCORE:			
Conformor			
A	B	C	D
69	62	42	27

As you may remember, she eventually found another job in research, but not without suffering a four-month period of anger, bewilderment, and denial.

Implementers and the Right Work Environment

Implementers are productive and content when they have some freedom to act according to their own style but within defined parameters. They like choice but only among limited options. They want someone to consult with rather than to risk going out on a limb. *Implementers* work best in what I call a *Directive* work environment.

A *Directive* work environment allows some shared responsibility, but it sets priorities and goals. It also indicates, though it may not always prescribe, the appropriate process for achieving them. It limits creativity selectively, and it limits change. Information about company business outside of the *Implementer's* immediate task is not offered but is accessible to those employees who want it and seek it out. The *Directive* environment can be found in a variety of organizations, both small and large. However, the organization cannot be small to the point where each individual is an island with no support system and no mechanism for sharing ideas and responsibilities. A theater company or a symphony might be an example of a *Directive* environment; creativity is allowed but there is always a script or

Implementers are productive and content when they have some freedom to act according to their own style but within defined parameters.

score and a director who pays close attention to detail. A *Directive* environment gives some freedom in schedule, space, and style but sets limits. For example, in one company, employees were allowed to decorate their workspace to suit themselves, but they had to choose from certain paint color samples and three furniture arrangements. They had more freedom to customize their workspace than they would have had in a *Bureaucratic* environment, but they were not free to bring in their own furnishings or to choose colors outside of the corporate palette.

Implementers are uncomfortable in highly-charged, competitive environments or in jobs where individuals are expected to achieve independently with very little oversight. They are also uncomfortable with too close supervision.

Implementers in the Wrong Work Environment — More Cautionary Tales

Tyler was an example of an *Implementer* misemployed in a *Bureaucratic* environment. He was a helpful young man who worked in customer service for a utility company. He was what the customers wanted: a helpful, friendly person who would listen to their problems and then use some initiative to solve them. The trouble was the company had a list of four and only four standardized responses the customer service reps

Implementers are uncomfortable in highly-charged, competitive environments.

were to give to callers: the repair specialist will arrive before ___ o'clock; let me transfer you to (another number); and so forth. The four responses worked efficiently for the company. That was not the case for Tyler. He sometimes revised or tailored the four responses in order to solve the customer's problem. The company was not prepared to work this way; nobody's forms fit Tyler's suggestions; nobody's job description could execute what he thought should be done. Tyler's coworkers could stay inside the four responses, why couldn't he? He was labeled the problem child. So he was fired. I got him in outplacement.

TYLER'S HIGHEST SCORE:			
Implementer			
A	B	C	D
46	(69)	57	28

After understanding that his desire to help was not bad, but he needed some flexibility, he took a job in customer service for a commercial catering firm. As an *Implementer* he was inbounds enough to follow the looser guidelines required for profitability, but innovative enough for a creative industry that wins customers by acquiescing to whims. Note that an *Innovator* in this job would give away the store; a *Conformer* would not be flexible enough. Tyler was exactly right for this job.

While Tyler had been an *Implementer* in a too confining *Bureaucratic* environment, Allison was an *Implementer* mismatched in the other direction.

ALLISON'S HIGHEST SCORE:			
Implementer			
A	B	C	D
44	(66)	51	39

Allison's family was in the retail clothing business. Her father had started the most successful store of this type in their city and as each of her brothers came of age, they opened another store in neighboring communities. Being an entrepreneur was the family's highest goal; being a person without a boss was her father's idea of having arrived. When it came Allison's turn she outperformed her brothers. She didn't open a new store in her father's business but left college after three years to start her own business as a printing broker. She had learned a good deal about this by observing the printing of brochures and ads and flyers for her father's business. She also liked the structure of the printing business — unlike retail clothing — it depended relatively little on fashion and taste but instead on how

well certain things were done. Allison was different from her father, and she was happy to have a
different area in which to be her own boss.
When she started out, her father was her first
customer. He was proud. She worked very hard
and grew the business. She later moved to another, faster growing city for a wider market.

One day she awoke not wanting to get out of
bed. Then she realized that she hadn't wanted to
get out of bed for quite some time. She was tired.
She took a day's vacation — the first time she
had done this — in order to have some quiet
time. She worked on some projects around her
house, tidied up some photographs, installed an
upgrade on her computer, hemmed a dress she
had bought previously and never worn. She had
such a feeling of quiet satisfaction that she wondered if she would ever want to sell again. She
was tired of selling. She wished she had a quiet
place to accomplish some things. She found a
card she had received at a Kiwanis Club meeting
where I had given a speech about career satisfaction. Then she phoned the speaker — who happened to be me — for an appointment.

After giving Allison a battery of assessment
tests, I discovered that she was far from an
Entrepreneurial personality. She didn't like risk.
She was highly structured, task-oriented; she
liked to do things her own way — she was not a
Conformer — but she had none of the characteristics of a salesperson. Yet, here she was selling all

day and in addition, running her own business. No wonder she was tired!

She had succeeded by sheer ambition and discipline; she made herself go sell every day. She was worn down and out.

At that time, The Mulling Companies needed someone in-house to take over the accounting function which was being outsourced. Since she had managed her own business and was a hard worker, I thought she might do very well setting up our accounting system. This was a structured job without any risk, but one where she could take full charge and tailor it to the needs of the company. She could create her own environment. Now, I am naturally an *Abdicator* boss, and I knew she was an *Implementer* and would need more direction than I was inclined to give. Knowing this, when she asked to schedule a meeting once a week with me, I readily agreed. Allison got a software package, set up an accounting system, asked for resources and created her own structured environment. She had just enough autonomy, as well as the reduced stress of no risk and no selling. Therefore, after correcting for a mismatched environment, there was a happy ending.

Only that wasn't the end. Allison made one more correction, this time in her choice of another element of the equation for optimal employment. She changed her work. About the time my company had grown to the point of needing a CFO full time to head up the accounting, Allison came to me with news. Her father, who had died the previous year, had left her a significant inheritance that allowed her to pursue her first love: music. She had taken voice and piano throughout her childhood, practiced for long hours, majored in voice in college, but quit to go into business. (Her family thought singing was not a business.) Now she could return to her music. Allison and her husband moved to a city known as a "music center" city where she composes music and coaches performers.

Participators and the Right Work Environment

Taking on new responsibilities in a changing or refocusing corporation is comfortable for the *Participator*. If you are a *Participator*, risk and ambiguity are stimulating to you as long as they are shared by others. You are responsible, but you don't want to be solely responsible. Teamwork and open communication are important and motivate the confident *Participator*. You need to have the ear of management when you want, but not constant attention. If you're a *Participator*, you work best in a *Democratic* work environment.

A *Democratic* work environment delegates responsibility freely. It encourages creativity and pride of ownership in employees and connects their accomplishments to the overall good of the

Teamwork and open communication are important and motivate the confident Participator.

Participators don't enjoy working alone or taking sole responsibility for decision-making.

company. *Democratic* environments reward some risk-taking by employees, but prefer employees to have checks and balances. A *Democratic* environment has more openness than either the *Bureaucratic* or *Directive*. Information is readily shared. Flextime might be a possibility and even telecommuting. Making appointments with superiors might not require a lot of advance notice. Employees could make "you handle Thursday for me and I'll take Friday for you" arrangements without going through administrative procedures. The work environment sought by the *Participator* can be found in many large and small organizations. However, the work environment must be large enough to allow the ebb and flow of ideas as well as to create the sense of shared purpose that *Participators* need to flourish.

A software company that must constantly develop new products or upgrade existing ones would typically have a *Democratic* environment, encouraging a free flow of ideas and valuing almost everyone's input. A project management team, the editorial staff of a magazine, or a publishing company would probably exemplify a *Democratic* environment. Employees in such a setting would brainstorm and innovate, although execution of big decisions would require approval from above.

Participators don't enjoy working alone or taking sole responsibility for decision-making.

They need to avoid work environments that are either too stringently or too loosely directed.

Participators in the Wrong Work Environment

As a dramatic example, the late Diana, Princess of Wales, was probably a *Participator*. In any case, she was mismatched in the epitome of the *Bureaucratic* environment — centuries old, protocol-driven Buckingham palace.

Princess Diana didn't have sufficient devotion to duty and routine, and she misunderstood the function of marriage in the royal structure. She was too flamboyant; she upstaged her superiors, appearing to go against the *Bureaucratic* pecking order. She was soon miserable and had disrupted the royal family.

Since you're unlikely to be in such a high-profile mismatch, you may relate more easily to the following tale about a *Participator*.

Randy was a strategic planner for the data processing function of a Fortune 500 company. No matter what the overall company environment was, the subculture of this support department was *Directive*. Why? Because its function was to respond to the needs of management for planning and decision-making rather than to create its own agenda. Such an environment was too confining for a *Participator* like Randy. He was not only brilliant, he was becoming more

*A **Participator** can be misemployed in an environment with too little structure where he doesn't receive the little bit of guidance he needs to use his talents best.*

and more strategically aggressive. After all, he had been in that department for fifteen years, he knew more than the others, and therefore, felt he could "get out of the box." He had always been too much of a risk-taker for that environment, but, as the company grew and its Information Resources Department became more structured and more integrated into the whole, the mismatch became more pronounced.

RANDY'S HIGHEST SCORE:			
Participator			
A	B	C	D
20	43	(79)	58

Finally, Randy began to push for a new Information Resources system, one that would capture the information for inventory control and distribution. It would, Randy believed, change the way the company did business. He believed that the new system would meet the needs of the future much better than the present one. The idea of revamping the entire system sounded like progress to Randy. It sounded like a huge and unnecessary expense to the company management, which was more worried about this year's profit/loss than something that might happen a decade down the road. The company, which fifteen years earlier had attracted Randy by its fluidity, was now in a holding mode. Randy debated the issues with his superiors at every opportunity until he became a thorn in their side. They sent him to me for executive coaching. I was supposed to help him "fit in better."

Much to the satisfaction of his employer, when Randy saw the problem as a mismatch of styles, he opted to move to another company rather than try to adapt. He now works for a smaller, less established firm that is eager to try Randy's new system as one means of positioning itself for the future.

While many *Participators* are misemployed in an environment that gives them too little room for creativity and flexibility, a *Participator* can be misemployed in an environment with too little structure where he doesn't receive the little bit of guidance he needs to use his talents best.

Gina was a New York public relations writer who had freelanced while her children were growing up, writing public relations pieces for business clients. Every one of her clients was delighted at how well she captured their style. She could get into any mood the client needed; it almost appeared that she read their minds.

One of her clients was an antique dealer on a grand scale; his twice-yearly showing of new wares were lavish extravaganzas. Customers came not only to buy but to be entertained. Gina had written several pieces on this entrepreneur; describing his shows that he portrayed in his PR

Participators want to share the responsibility.

GINA'S HIGHEST SCORE:			
Participator			
A	B	C	D
39	48	(65)	48

kit. At one point she had suggested some nice touches to his spring show's "April in Paris" theme, and he was impressed. Consequently, he asked if she would take the theme and finish the job. Gina created a Folies-Bergère scene at one side of the showroom complete with a chorus line of can-can girls. She also created a Montmartre scene on the other side of the space and scattered easels along the "sidewalks" where customers could dabble with real paints. The entrepreneur liked it so much that he had wanted models to pose outdoors. Gina drafted a couple of dancers to stand on make-shift window ledges for the "artists" to use as models to paint. She had rather enjoyed working outdoors and in a different environment. He was amazed at how she made his vision come true.

Because of this success, she asked the antique dealer if she could be his full time PR person. She chose his operation because it appeared more creative than her corporate clients.

Once Gina was actually on board, however, she discovered a very unstructured environment. Nobody seemed to know who did what in the

business; the employees were all acting independently. The closest thing to a title was "sort of
my assistant," and, if there were any policies, they
were decided after hours and nobody knew what
any of them were. Gina wondered about the
extravagant stories describing each of the
antiques and if any of them were documented.
She began to wonder if the "royal bed" that she
was writing about in the press releases had ever
really belonged to royalty. This operation was not
retail; it was entertainment, and rules did not
seem to apply.

The owner had one goal: not just to be
known in the city, but to be notorious. He wanted events and publicity to achieve that goal.
Where before he had hired Gina to develop
projects already selected, now he wanted her to
come up with her own projects — constantly.
Her creativity seemed to flee, and she shot down
her own ideas without pursuing them.

Gina finally realized that, although she
thought of herself as creative, she enjoyed flesh-
ing out ideas rather than creating them. The boss
who had given her direction as a freelancer was
always busy with other things now that she was
in charge. What had seemed exciting when she
was on the outside, now made Gina cringe. She
had been living in one big cringe for months.
She really didn't want to work in this environment, but she felt like a failure to quit her very
first full time job.

Finally, the owner came to her, saying sternly, "I need three off-the-wall events between now and the year's end, and I need to know what the concepts will be by next Monday." She went out in the parking lot and cried. She soon decided that this was a good time to move to another city where her daughter lived and to seek career consulting.

"I was happy freelancing," she said, "but I wanted more steady pay; so the job with the antique dealer appeared to be the dream job. I had already done his work so well. What's wrong with me now?"

There was nothing wrong with Gina. She was creative enough to be a PR writer and enough of a self-starter to do it freelance; but, being a *Participator*, she wasn't a risk taker. *Participators* want to share the responsibility. She wanted to be able to brainstorm with someone, get feedback, and arrive at a consensus. She didn't want it to come down to just her. She was also a pleaser; and she needed someone to please along the way. It did not suit her to work alone until the final results. Finally, she was not flamboyant, and she did not want to be on the edge as far as rules of propriety or truth were concerned.

In the end, Gina got a job on a magazine staff in her new town, writing about antiques and decorative arts. There she had an editor and other staff to use as a sounding board, editorial meetings and guidelines, but also a lot of free-dom. She also had a new topic and new contacts to make every month to keep things interesting.

Innovators in the Right Work Environment

Innovators thrive in environments that are open to new approaches. To be satisfied, they require almost absolute control over their particular areas of responsibility. If you're an *Innovator*, you're likely to be a risk-taker who thrives on uncertainty, unpredictability, and risk in a rapid-ly growing company. You're very comfortable with start-up situations or in organizations undergoing dramatic restructuring or change. You'll do best in an *Entrepreneurial* environment.

An *Entrepreneurial* environment is one where aggressive, independent-minded, often outspoken thinkers are regarded as valuable assets. It gives broad responsibility to independ-ent people who don't like tight controls over their work.

In an *Entrepreneurial* environment, policies and procedures — when there are any — seem to always be barely ahead or slightly behind what's actually happening. Parking and other privileges are on a first come, first served basis. Pecking order is what you make of it. *Entrepreneurial* environments have no rules about such things as

An Entrepreneurial environment gives broad responsibility to independent people who don't like tight controls over their work.

> Everyone thinks of changing the world, but no one thinks of changing himself.
>
> **Leo Tolstoy**

decorating your work space. I know a law firm where every partner has done his office in a different and personal style. You walk down the hall and see an office with plaid wallpaper and a western theme next to an office with silk flowers and oriental vases next to one with hunt scenes and heavy mahogany furniture. Each partner has his own niche, his own clientele, and his own style. That's *Entrepreneurial*.

If you hear someone in the hall say, "Let's close on Veteran's Day this year. We're usually open but let's just close this year."

And someone answers, "Yeah okay," then you know you are probably in an *Entrepreneurial* environment. Word will go out by e-mail that the company will be closed. A few people don't pick up the message; but, hey, that's their responsibility.

In an *Entrepreneurial* environment, people make decisions intuitively — "Let's give them a 4% raise," someone says.

"No, that's a little low. Let's give them 4½%."

And the first person says, "Okay. Let's do it." They know that if they study the matter, the opportunity will be gone. They know there's a risk in flying by the seat of their pants, but when their move works, it's great. If it doesn't, they don't look back. "We took a chance," they say and go on to the next one. The key here is that the

Entrepreneurial environment encourages this kind of behavior.

In *Entrepreneurial* environments, lots of people come up with ideas and they all come together — or they don't — but things are always moving. Information is in the air you breathe. You don't have to ask for information to be pulled from some private file. It's "out there" and everybody's talking about it. An *Entrepreneurial* environment typically has an accelerated product development cycle. And if a more conservative company has a department with an *Entrepreneurial* subculture, that department will by-pass controls. For example, someone gets an idea and doesn't send it through the prescribed channels; they may outsource parts of it. Where it would take the regular routine more than a year to develop a new product after studying the market and doing the financial projections, these folks can develop, repackage, and present a new product to a potential client in a few weeks. They sometimes get in trouble, but they often get a jump on the market and beat out the competition.

An *Entrepreneurial* environment is likely to be found in advertising companies, outside sales divisions, new product development departments, literary agencies, and small start-up companies. It's hard for a big company to be *Entrepreneurial*, but there are occasional exceptions. One such example is Home Depot, which

*If a more conservative company has a department with an **Entrepreneurial** subculture, that department will by-pass controls.*

The Entrepreneurial environment is least often found in large, old companies, and more often found in new, growing ones.

manages loosely and empowers store salespersons to train customers. This company also fosters a feeling of ownership; almost every employee has stock in the company. While the *Entrepreneurial* environment can be found in both small and large organizations, it is least often found in large, old companies, and more often found in new, growing ones.

If your scores from **The Mulling Factor** label you an *Innovator*, beware of stable, predictable corporate cultures that use "tried and true" methods and cautious approaches to problem-solving or strategic decision-making. You won't thrive in an environment where you must conform to rules, or work carefully, sharing responsibility for success or failure with other individuals or team members. Politically-oriented, *Bureaucratic*, tightly-controlled corporate cultures will be intolerable to you.

Innovators in the Wrong Work Environment

General Douglas MacArthur, while commander of the forces in Korea in 1950, wanted to invade Mainland China; but this action was forbidden by his superiors. In 1951 MacArthur was fired by President Truman, not for military missteps but because the General criticized U.S. policy and Truman's leadership. MacArthur was an *Innovator* in an organization, the military, in which the chain of command may not be violated and in which loyalty is required. The general was popular, successful, but rightly fired, a fate which befalls many *Innovators* who have risen to the top outside of their ideal work environment.

Like the General, Dennis was something of a renegade. His company sent him out to foreign operations where he was highly successful at making deals and putting out fires. He knew how to get things done in the most difficult political situations, sometimes by creative solutions, sometimes by mislabeling a few expenditures and using the freed-up money as "incentives" to smooth the way. He often stepped on toes, doing what was needed to get the job done. He was an *Innovator* all the way.

After a series of successful turn-arounds, the company wanted to settle down into a more "civilized" operation and Dennis was no longer their guy. The company brought Dennis back to the corporate office, a *Directive* environment where he would have to cooperate. Dennis thought the company wanted him where they could keep him under their thumb. Actually, nobody wanted him at all. He had burned bridges with almost every-

> When patterns are broken, new worlds can emerge.
> **Tuli**
> **Kupferberg**

In many companies, the work environment is a creation or extension of the boss.

DENNIS' HIGHEST SCORE:			
Innovator			
A	B	C	D
39	48	48	(65)

one there, even from a distance. Nobody but Dennis actually expected this to work. They sent him to me to help determine where he would fit. They not-so-secretly hoped Dennis would see that he didn't fit into this company at all, and they got their wish. Dennis is now an overseas consultant, a turn-around specialist for hire. Now he can burn all his bridges in a company to fix the low profit situation and never look back, and that's just the way he likes it.

If Dennis, an *Innovator* brought into a *Directive* environment, was mismatched, even more out of place was Juanita, one of the most creative and independent individuals I've ever met, an *Innovator* from the word go. She has been very successful working in a small, family-owned architectural firm.

Seeking to expand her experience and her horizons, she went to work for a larger, very *Bureaucratic* firm. It was a disaster from day one. Literally. She began doing things without asking her boss' permission. She began streamlining the way vendors did business with her new company, making what appeared to be radical changes

JUANITA'S HIGHEST SCORE:			
Innovator			
A	B	C	D
22	36	66	(76)

practically overnight. The changes she made were positive but were made much too quickly for the environment.

Juanita's most critical mistake: not only did she not consult her *Controller* boss, she never tried to win over her colleagues. Her co-workers began to resent her because they liked working for a strong authority figure who made all the decisions. This created a risk-free, not a risk-taking environment for them.

When Juanita finally tried to sell the boss or her co-workers on a brilliant idea, they had become so alienated they refused to listen or take her seriously. The harder she tried to sell herself to the *Controller* boss, the worse the situation became. Juanita, a clear *Innovator*, made the mistake of working for a non-empowering *Controller* boss in a predictable *Bureaucratic* work environment. She was terminated within ninety days and branded a total misfit when, in fact, she was only mismatched with her work environment.

This firm was cohesive until Juanita came along, and it returned to unity when Juanita left.

In a Less Than Ideal World

As you have undoubtedly guessed, there is often a close relationship between the boss and the work environment. In many companies, the

> I can't change the direction of the wind, but I can adjust my sails to always reach my destination.
> **Jimmy Dean**

work environment is a creation or extension of the boss. In fact, in the boss' absence, the work environment acts as boss. For instance, in the utilities company where Tyler, the customer service representative, had previously worked ... if the boss was on vacation the customer reps continued to give their four prescribed responses. No problem. Likewise, whether the *Abdicator* boss is in or not, the understanding that employees are on their own prevails.

So, in an ideal world, a *Controller* boss presides over a *Bureaucratic* environment, a *Coach* is boss in a *Director* environment, a *Delegator* is in charge in a *Democratic* environment, and an *Abdicator* is head of an *Entrepreneurial* environment.

Unfortunately, it's not an ideal world. Your boss may be misemployed — after all, many people are. A boss mismatched with the environment means an unhappy boss and, to some degree, a mismatch for you. You may feel jerked back and forth between the two.

Determining what your needs are, as you have done through **The Mulling Factor**, then sizing up your boss and the work environment — that is, recognizing the source and degree of your mismatch — are the first critical steps toward achieving contentment on the job. Knowing the source of your discomfort may relieve some of your distress. To achieve your greatest possible

A boss mismatched with the environment means an unhappy boss and, to some degree, a mismatch for you.

happiness, however, you must take charge of your destiny.

This may mean leaving your current unfulfilling job and finding not just a new job, but the correct job. Or it may mean turning the job you have into the most suitable job for you. Yes, there are ways to manage your boss to insure that he or she will give you what you want. And there are ways to create your own ideal sub-culture within the larger one. Your challenge now is to decide which way to go, whether to leave or to reshape your job. The next chapter will help you make that decision.

BUILDING *THE MULLING FACTOR*
CHART 3

You: *Conformer*	Your Best Boss: *Controller*	Your Best Environment: *Bureacratic*
consistent	hands on	policy-driven
dependable	looks over shoulder	regulated
cautious	checks work	uniform
orderly	monitors set procedures	established
compliant	expects no input from you	requires permission to act
loyal	firm	slow to change
precise	fair	clear chain of command

You: *Implementer*	Your Best Boss: *Coach*	Your Best Environment: *Directive*
helpful	teaches	limted change
organized	directs	innovation within rules
uncompetitive	steps in often	allows some input
productive	listens to you	access to information
careful	motivates	
committed	sets goals	
practical	assigns roles	
	establishes procedures	
	supports you	

BUILDING *THE MULLING FACTOR*
CHART 3 (Continued)

You: *Participator*	Your Best Boss: *Delegator*	Your Best Environment: *Democratic*
flexible	sets over-all goals	responsive to employee input
responsive	leaves methods to you	changing
assertive	steps in when you ask	exchanges information
persuasive	requires infrequent reports	shares accountability
sharing risk	advises	encourages teamwork
communicative	challenges you	
open to ambiguity	receptive to your ideas	
	encourages self-development	

You: *Innovator*	Your Best Boss: *Abdicator*	Your Best Environment: *Entreprenurial*
independent	rarely present	reacts quickly
risk-taking	strategic thinker	values new ideas
motivated by change	hands-off	encourages risk
creative	trusts you to do the job	growing
self-starting	empowering	unpredictable
confrontive	focuses on results	rapidly changing
convincing	decides quickly	few established policies
adventurous	expects self-development	information-rich

When to Hold 'Em, When to Fold 'Em

Are you a match with your current boss?

If two men on a job agree all the time, then one is useless. If they disagree all the time, then both are useless.

Darryl F. Zanuck

NOW YOU KNOW your preferred work-ing style — and the type of boss and work environment that make the best match with your style. Are you a match with your current boss? If you're like most people, the answer is "no." You aren't working in your best-fit situation. You're mismatched and misemployed.

What can you do about it?

You could leave. You could throw in your hat and start looking for the type of boss and envi-ronment *The Mulling Factor* identified for you.

Leaving is always an option, but it's not always the best one. Sometimes staying in the game makes sense. Perhaps a family member is in poor health and is depending on your group medical insurance. Perhaps you're only one year away from being 100% vested in the company pension plan. Maybe your boss is about to retire or the company is about to merge or reorganize and you have reason to believe you will benefit from that event. If you have a career plan, and I hope you do, you may need more work experience in your current job to be fully prepared to achieve your future goals. That was once my case. As a Human Resources professional, I deliberately spent three years in a company that was not a good fit for me in order to get union experience before I went on to my targeted position. Typically, you tolerate a mismatch for a short period of time in your early jobs while you are learning the ropes. A consciously chosen, temporary mismatch for a good reason is altogether different from misemployment that you haven't identified, can't control, and have no hope of leaving.

Do you want to evaluate your options with a cooler head?

Through **The Mulling Factor**, you know why you're so stressed and why you and your boss seem so far apart. It's not the personality conflict you thought it was. It's not that she's the jerk you were sure she was. Her style just doesn't match yours. It's not a personal thing at all. Knowing this, you can let go of that anger and frustration you've been feeling about the job, stand back, and evaluate your options with a cooler head.

Option One: Endure

Enduring is what you've been doing. You may be able to endure even longer. But there's always a price — stress and unhappiness. So, while enduring might be a necessary evil in some cases, don't talk yourself into doing nothing by saying, "Oh, it's not so bad," simply because you don't want to face a change. A high level of tolerance, in fact, stands in the way of positive change.

Option Two: Adapt

If you do decide to stay, everything doesn't have to stay the same. You don't have to simply endure your misemployment. You can act upon it in a positive way. You, yourself, can adapt and/or you can manage your boss.

Adapting means changing your style to give your boss what he or she wants. It means using *The Mulling Factor* to identify behaviors that will make you fit better into your boss' supervisory style. Remember: you've not only discovered that you've got the wrong boss; you've also discovered that your boss has the wrong employee! *The Mulling Factor* tells you what he needs and you need. Adapting to your boss' style gets you something you want and/or need; for example, you keep your job, you benefit from your boss' improved approval and from his success. But adapting to make your boss happier, though it has its rewards, should usually be a short-term approach if it doesn't result in your needs being met as well.

For too long, it was taken for granted that it was the boss' responsibility to create, define, and set the tone of the employer/employee relationship.

Option Three: Manage Your Boss

The best approach, especially for the long haul, is to manage your boss to insure that your needs are met too. It's worth a try. And it's up to you. For too long, it was taken for granted that it was the boss' responsibility to create, define, and set the tone of the employer/employee relationship. Not true. I hold that this critical relationship is the subordinate's responsibility, because, realistically, if it doesn't work out, it's the employee who suffers the most.

Take control of your situation now because a mismatch of styles, which begins with mutual misunderstanding, may eventually deteriorate to personal hostility. Once a mismatch "gets personal," it's harder to manage.

The people who are happiest in their careers are those who have the ideal boss or who have learned how to manage their boss in such a way that will cause this boss to resemble their ideal one.

Naturally, if you're an *Innovator* and your boss is a *Controller*, your styles are far from meshing. Two whole types on *The Mulling Factor* chart lie between your ideal boss and your actual boss. If each of you could move an entire type toward each other, your styles still would not match. That might be too far to go.

However, if you and your boss are off by only one style ... say, he's an *Abdicator* and you're a *Participator*, or you're an *Implementer* and she's

How does your boss like to be approached? Do you even know?

a *Delegator* … you may very well work out a meeting of the styles. An adjustment by both of you might lead you to common ground.

In judging whether the gap is too great to bridge, there are several variables to consider besides the distance of the gap: your flexibility, your boss' response, and how motivated you are to make the mismatch work.

Remember also that some types are more flexible than others. One of the basic characteristics of a *Participator*, for example, is flexibility, so a *Participator* would probably have an easier time meeting a less-than-ideal boss than, for example, a *Conformer* would. Similarly, a particular boss might be totally unwilling to adjust his management style while another, even of the same type, might be willing to give it a try.

When is your boss' most receptive time?

How To Get Your Boss To Change Without Getting Fired

If you're asking for change in your boss' behavior, you need to approach them in the way most palatable to them (not to you). How does your boss like to be approached? Do you even know? Are they seemingly just a bundle of unpredictable moods and hair trigger responses? Have you taken the time to find out?

Using Small Talk Effectively

Use "small talk" effectively to get to know your boss. Chat on the elevator, at lunch, while waiting for colleagues to gather for a meeting. But don't chat about yourself, chat about them. Ask polite questions about their hometown, their alma mater, their children, their hobbies. Try active listening to encourage them to talk about themselves. Mention the things that interest them at later times, thus, showing that you remember. People like people who take an interest in them. Being liked may be your biggest advantage in asking your boss to change for your comfort. And the more you know what makes your boss tick, the more you know how to approach them with your requests and input.

At the Best Time in the Best Place

Asking your boss seriously for any change in an arena critical to your job performance deserves the optimal time and place. What is your boss' "best" time? I'm not saying when is his most productive time — that may be the time he wants to get his major work of the day accomplished and be undisturbed, or it may be his most "hyper" time when he wouldn't want to slow down to consider your request. I'm asking when is his most receptive time? When is he relaxed, open, interested, and friendly — or as close to these states as he ever gets? The answers are highly individual.

For example, if your boss is a smoker in a non-smoking environment, his smoking break may be the best time and place to talk to him. He takes that one long first drag on the cigarette and immediately the world looks better to him. Be there then. It's not for nothing that people do business out back on the loading dock.

Often the best time is after the others have left work and your boss is still there. Just as often, however, that's the worst time, when he is frustrated trying to get some essentials done before he rushes home. Sometimes lunch works best — that might mean when the others are out and he's alone eating a sandwich at his desk, or it might mean going with him to a nice restaurant for lunch. Or maybe he takes personnel affairs so seriously that prime is first thing Monday morning. You will only know by watching. See when and where the boss seems most optimistic, tuned-in, and responsive to other people; and act accordingly.

I have recently read a biography by Richard Hyatt, *Zell, The Governor Who Gave Georgia Hope* (about the former Governor of Georgia and current U.S. Senator, Zell Miller), who, in his very first campaign to represent his home county in the state legislature, went door to door asking for votes. The young man went to all the "gettables," those who were neither solidly for him nor solidly against him. There's nothing unusual about that. What is unusual is that he went to their houses before they were out of bed in the morning. He would awaken them, which was considered a compliment, have breakfast with them, and at this point, ask for their vote. Governor Miller also added that late at night also worked for this technique.

The twenty-eight year old Miller won a seat in the Georgia State Senate representing an area previously tied up by a political boss. He did it by picking the right time and place to get his voter's favorable attention. I advise you to do the same. I obviously don't mean that you wake the boss up before dawn, I mean know your audience.

One way of managing your boss—the one you should consider first—is simply to ask him to change. Can you do that?

Communicating in the Boss' Preferred Style

Knowing your boss' preferred communication style is as important as knowing his best time and place. First, is he visual or auditory? Does he say, "Tell me …," or does he say, "Show me …?" Does he call for graphs, computer printouts or spreadsheets and annual reports in considering other important matters? Or does he wave these away?

Is he more impressed by long reports with data to prove everything, or does he prefer people who "cut to the chase?" Is he detailed-oriented, or does he become impatient with details and

Don't wear out your welcome. want only the big picture or the bottom line? Give him what he wants.

One way of managing your boss — the way you should consider first — is simply to ask him to change. At the right time and place, tell him what you need to work more productively and, especially, TO MEET HIS EXPECTATION BETTER. First, present your need for more, less or different supervision in a general way.

The most direct approach, of course, is to give your boss this book and ask him to read it. This would allow you to be able to discuss your relationship in *The Mulling Factor* terms. But even here, think. Would you hand your boss the whole book or a chapter from it, or would it be best to hand him just the chart of descriptive words at the end of Chapters Three, Four, and Five? Do what fits his communication style, not what represents yours. Give him what he will actually absorb.

Let this sink in. Then, at a later time, be more specific. But don't overwhelm him. Because of what you have learned through *The Mulling Factor*, you can target those behaviors that define the gap between you and the boss. Leave the rest alone.

Outline some changes in amount, type, and frequency of instruction, feedback, or reward and seek his agreement. When both of you know what you're trying to achieve, there is more chance for success.

If you feel you can't ask your boss for a fundamental change in your relationship or if you tried and failed, go to plan B: manage the boss more subtly. Shape his behavior by changing yours. Here are a few specific ways presented according to the individual styles.

Conformers Manage the Boss

If you're a *Conformer*, you'll very likely need to manage a boss who is less guiding than you require. It is your responsibility to get what you need at each step of a project while giving the boss as little to do as possible.

From the beginning, you need detailed, specific instructions given one step at a time. You want your boss' expectations expressed in terms of each small step of the task. Tell your boss you do not feel at ease without some intermediate goals. This identifies you in terms of your supervisory needs. If he's willing to try to meet them, fine. Ask if he'll meet with you on a regular basis. Make it as few as possible, say once a week. If he agrees, then write down in advance of each meeting what you need to know that will provide you with the most direction possible.

In addition to direction, you want feedback after you have completed each step, not just at the end. "Is this okay?" you often say during a project. You want "partial credit" for steps done well.

Suppose you must develop a shipping schedule to send to suppliers. Typically the *Abdicator* or *Delegator* boss will not ask to see it. She assumes you'll do it right and put it to use or send it out. You, however, feel in limbo without her commenting on it and giving the OK before it goes out.

Approaching her directly, you say, "I need to cover this with you." If she takes the schedule and begins to look at it, take whatever response you get. Don't wear out your welcome. Get your approval and suggestions quickly and leave. Don't tell her how you arrived at each point on the schedule or "wonder" things out loud with her.

If you're an **Implementer** *working with a* **Controller** *boss, you may feel mismatched because you have a boss who is looking too closely over your shoulder every step of the way.*

If she doesn't seem inclined to look at the schedule or, if you are unwilling to initiate the interaction this directly, you could send her the schedule attached to an e-mail or memo — short, because that's what she requires — saying, "Here's the schedule. If I hear nothing from you, I'll assume you're OK with it and I'll send it out at five o'clock tomorrow." Then silence must mean approval and the *Conformer* will have to take it as such. The boss will also be prompted to consider the chart and may note possible improvements, something she might not otherwise have done. By getting the boss to consider the schedule one way or another, you will have moved her, at least, from an *Abdicator* to a *Delegator* in behavior. (And if she never looks at the chart and does not contact you, that e-mail has covered your tracks.)

Remember Phil, the shy financial analyst who was trying to schedule meetings with his *Abdicator* boss to approve and direct his every step? In this *Conformer/Abdicator* mismatch, Phil was terrified he'd do something wrong without her input. Short of finding another boss, he needed to manage the one he had. He had to make it his business to get a clear understanding of her expectations. He had to convince her to set specifications and guidelines that were structured enough for him to comprehend and use. Phil's guidance would have decreased the risk of his delivering the wrong results, reducing the fear that held him back. As it turned out, she not only didn't want to tell Phil how to accomplish his tasks, she didn't know how. She didn't know the steps. If she knew the steps, maybe she wouldn't need him. So she was unwilling and/or unable to accommodate. This is often the case. But is it hopeless?

The Surrogate Boss

There is one avenue left to try before throwing in the towel and getting a new job. Find an intermediary or mentor, or the surrogate boss. Often, the boss' assistant may understand and respond well to your need. Another supervisor at your boss' level or closer to yours may be willing to give you direction and feedback. Even a peer can be helpful.

I'm an *Abdicator* boss myself, in an *Entrepreneurial* environment. I'm thinking of a *Conformer* who does beautiful work for me as a word processor. I have every respect for the work she does, especially because it deals with endless details I would not have the patience to even think about. When I need her to do something for me, I don't go directly to her for that very reason. I describe the results I want to someone else and ask that person — a more hands-on type boss, a *Controller* or *Coach* — to give instruction and feedback to the word-processor until she has my work finished. I give her reward/approval only when I have the finished product in my hands. She has succeeded with an *Abdicator* boss — by virtue of a surrogate boss, and she has created her own subculture in the support office apart from the mainstream of our business.

Implementers Manage the Boss

If you're an *Implementer* working with a *Controller* boss, you may feel mismatched because you have a boss who is looking too closely over your shoulder every step of the way.

You need to arrange to meet the boss less often than he would naturally expect. Say directly to him, "Could we go over this step and the next step now so I can be looking ahead?" You

sound eager, but what you have in mind is that if
you do two steps today, you won't have to meet
again over the second step.

Have an agenda.

If he agrees, pretend the boss is going on a
two-week vacation and talk to him as you would
if this were true. Your attitude will be, "When
you get back all of this will be done." Talk just
that way to him, except don't actually mention
the word "vacation."

Talk through where you are going next, and
then ask if you can talk about the next few steps
also. Ask him to give you a clear understanding
of how this will go. Take a deep breath while you
meet his needs to detail everything; listen and
nod. Then go about the next few steps without
his constant oversight — he's on vacation, right?
— skipping around among the steps or using
different techniques without his being aware.
When any step is done and out of the way, e-
mail your boss that it's completed. If he gets a
progress report as often as he would have met
with you, he most likely will be satisfied. In this
manner you make him very comfortable that
everything is covered while you buy yourself a
little autonomy.

On the other hand, suppose you, as an
Implementer, have an *Abdicator* or a *Delegator*
boss and you are not getting as much structure as
you need. Ask for more regular meetings with
your boss. Tell him that to be more productive
you need to touch base more often. If he grants

your request even once, then do him a favor and conduct the meeting as efficiently as possible. That's the only way he'll consider meeting on a regular basis.

Have an agenda. Not ten pages, just a short outline. Limit the topics to your two, three, or four most urgent ones. Write no more than four or six words per sub-topic, if any, to be discussed. Hand the agenda to the boss up front. A simple sheet of paper helps insure that your topics will be covered.

If you get even your top two concerns covered, you will be more satisfied. Your boss has moved toward fulfilling your needs. Now you try to change, thinking through the less critical concerns yourself.

If your request for regular meetings is denied, you will have to catch your *Delegator* or *Abdicator* boss "on the fly." Have one question at a time only and arrange to bump into him somewhere he's comfortable — waiting for the elevator, between meetings, or whenever you know he's loose — and run your concern by him.

If you still have questions, go to the surrogate boss, the boss' secretary, another supervisor,

Find a mentor to help you bridge the gap that still remains between your style and the boss'.

MAGGIE'S HIGHEST SCORE:			
Implementer			
A	B	C	D
52	(65)	43	40

or a peer who has insight into the steps of what you're trying to do. Find a mentor to help you bridge the gap that still remains between your style and the boss'.

Communication is the key.

Maggie has been a technician with an interior plant service business. She works for Alan who owns the company. He is a *Delegator* boss. He likes to get systems set up and then have them run smoothly. He gets very aggravated when subordinates call him with every little decision when he thinks they could decide themselves. His motto is "I don't want to hear about it unless I have to."

He is a good judge of character and he chooses people well; he is decisive and gets rid of bad apples quickly. Recently, he promoted Maggie, his best technician and a hard-working woman with common sense, to be a supervisor and trainer of technicians. He was very pleased with the situation.

Maggie was an *Implementer*. She knew her plants, her technicians, and her clients. She understood the consequences of reacting to special demands in any of these areas. She understood that she had the responsibility for the bread and butter work of the business, but she had not received direction from Alan as to how to do all this. He relied on her common sense to figure it out. But Maggie, unused to being a supervisor, lacked the confidence she needed. Every day clients would want change-outs, or the colors of plants were not as expected and the supplier had to be contacted, or construction in a client building prevented the regularly scheduled plant maintenance, or a technician's truck broke down. At first, Maggie would call Alan on these frequent occasions and he would snap, "Maggie, DEAL with it." But Maggie felt insecure in making decisions to reroute techs, shuffle trucks, reorder; she was afraid that after the fact he'd say they were the wrong decisions. She dreaded things going wrong. Her stress was such that she wanted to give up her promotion and go back to being a tech.

She scheduled a meeting to tell her boss about her needs — much better than just resigning without having voiced a complaint, as many people in her position would have done. When she explained how she felt without direction and shared her solution to this, he was horrified at the thought of losing her talents. He agreed to take some time to set up guidelines for dealing with each kind of disruption. For example, a plant can be dying without his hearing about it unless it's a specimen plant over five feet costing three hundred dollars or more. He prioritized problems and changes in routine and set up a hierarchy of procedures and people to call. Alan hated every minute of it; he was not a detail person, but he was highly motivated to change. And besides that, he expected to have to deal with this only once.

He also arranged for a beeper system that connected the techs to Maggie and Maggie to the greenhouse. He told her she was expected to beep the appropriate people, but he was not to be called except on occasions of a specified seriousness expressed in dollars or time or safety and/or liability issues. A traffic accident in which a technician is involved gets a beep; a truck breakdown with no liability does not. Maggie has the number of a road service and a towing company, and he expects her or the nearest tech to pick up the one stranded. He gave her specific (rather than implied) authority to act, told her it might occasionally involve mistakes, but he was prepared for that.

Do active listening...

Maggie is now dealing well with the unaccustomed position of supervisor. Alan protects himself from disruptions and only has to deal with overall marketplace factors, not the day-to-day operations.

Participators Manage the Boss

To mesh with the boss, who is more constricting than you would like, set up a format for each project — a chart or outline — and put it on your desk. Keep a sheet on your desk to take notes about each phone call or meeting or interaction you have during the day. At the end of the day, devote fifteen minutes to move your style towards your boss'. Go through the notes and

Each of us is responsible for accessing and correcting our own mismatches.

put a phrase about each interaction onto the form for the corresponding project. If your boss prefers narration to charts, these phrases can be strung together in sentences to make a daily paragraph, a journal of what's going on in your office. Stick each day's entry in your boss' mailbox as you leave or e-mail it or — if he is auditory — read it to him at the end of every day just before HE leaves. The boss will be so overwhelmed with the detail of your data that he will never bug you again. P.S. You might find the record useful yourself some day. Choosing to devote fifteen minutes a day to managing the boss is much less stressful than being bugged frequently during the day; it allows you to be in control.

If you still must take occasional detailed direction from the boss, sit and listen to him attentively and accept steps one, two, three, and so forth. Do active listening to each step; that is, repeat each step back to him naturally in your own words. What you get for this behavior is that he doesn't feel he needs to look over your shoulder.

You don't need such detailed direction, but you're accepting it to keep your boss happy, to give him what he needs in order to obtain what you need. It's more tolerable to sit for one hour a week while he tells you exactly what to do, knowing this is a deliberate adaptation on your part, than to be struggling all the time with the mismatch.

In Sherman's case, the boss adapted. Sherman needed more direction than he was getting from the owner of the architectural firm, and he felt adrift with no plan. The boss was an *Abdicator*. He had no intention of coaching Sherman; he just wanted the right results. But he did the next best thing. He hired me to do the executive coaching for him. Whatever works. If Sherman's boss had not seen the need, it would have been up to Sherman to ask the boss for access to outside help to remedy the problem. Each of us is responsible for assessing and correcting our own mismatches.

Innovators Manage the Boss

Being at the far end of the continuum, the *Innovator* has to stretch a lot to please a too-controlling boss.

An *Innovator* needs to be told only the end result expected and wants to be left to design their own steps to accomplish this. When the too-controlling boss starts in with the steps he wants you to follow, ask him to give you the expected results or goal first so you can put the steps into perspective. Tell him that, without the overall goal, you feel as if you are learning to play a new board game without knowing the object of the game. Someone says, "Put your game piece in these squares and then roll the dice and move one of the pieces four spaces," but you don't know what the object of the game is.

You really want to know if there are other options that will have the same results, and other better steps to accomplish it, but you come across as saying to your boss, "I will understand the steps better if you tell me the goal."

The more controlling the boss is, the more he wants to keep important information (like his overall strategy) close to the vest. But if you ask him directly, your boss may oblige. Then you will be free to play the game your way … as long as you keep him informed according to the steps of HIS game plan.

Keeping the boss informed is essential if you're going to live with a too-controlling boss.

Keeping the boss informed is essential if you're going to live with a too-controlling boss. You have an obligation to keep him involved. This boss must know whether or not you are meeting your goals and his expectations. For example, if you have six intermediate goals, you need to let the boss know if you are meeting, lagging behind or, hopefully, overachieving on each one.

Sherry was an *Innovator* who consulted me about getting along with a *Coach* boss who wanted to micromanage her. I told her to leave him a voice mail every day. Go directly into voice mail, don't let it ring because he might answer and you'd be in the middle of a micromanaging session. Just devote two minutes daily to this task

— the price you must pay for having a less than ideal boss. The price is far smaller than stress over constant concern with micromanaging.

As an *Innovator*, you have another concern. You want your rewards to be in the form of money and public praise. The ego is the operant force. You prefer your success to be widely publicized when possible. Money is not just to pay the bills, it also feeds your ego. CEO *Innovators* who earn millions of dollars still want more money in order to be able to move up the list of best-paid CEOs. Because money is how you keep score, you want more money for a job well done. You're willing to risk getting less money for a job that doesn't turn out as well. Bonuses that actually reflect performance motivate you as do commissions and percentages of deals. Ask for them. Show your boss how they will gain, not lose, by a pay-for-performance approach to your compensation. Obviously, you have to be in a work environment (or even a sub-culture) fairly close to *Entrepreneurial* to get this compensation package that is tailored to your needs for motivation.

And if you need more public credit to feel sufficiently rewarded, be your own publicity agent. Write up a short article about your recent successful project and submit it to the company newsletter or ask the PR Department to send it to the local business publication or newspaper. Offer your services as an expert source to your local press. There's nothing wrong with inducing someone else to toot your horn. It's called public relations, and it will benefit your company, too.

Also, giving the boss credit is another way an *Innovator* can manage the boss. Since an *Innovator* likes publicity for himself, it is a stretch for him to give credit to the boss. However, the people in the know — and aren't they the people who matter? — know where the credit belongs. Besides, its good exposure for you to praise someone else publicly, and doing it naturally really enhances rather than detracts from your own credit.

Let's look at Mike, The *Innovator* CEO of a start-up company who reported to the *Controller* CFO of the parent company. He took the start-up money, hired his own people, and set them free to attack the market aggressively. He saw no need to keep the CFO informed. When the CFO questioned him extensively at every meeting, Mike did not note the urgency and slipping confidence in his boss' voice. "I want to be informed," is what he was saying. If Mike had recognized the boss' need for an *Conformer* in this job, he could have satisfied the *Conformer's* behavior; he could have informed the boss of every candidate he was considering for his management team and sent their credentials to the CFO, underlining the ones that he considered most important to justify his choices. He could have sent frequent memos or e-mails to the boss

There's nothing wrong with inducing someone else to toot your horn.

about the progress of each new product or marketing strategy, expectations and results — in that way, the boss could see progress in figures and would have something to present to his own boss. Not only would frequent reporting allay the concerns of the CFO, it would make it easier for him to deal with his boss.

When To Play, and When To Throw in the Cards

In summary, you determine your needs. You determine your boss' needs. You determine the difference. You assess your desire and the boss' willingness to change in the three primary areas, as necessary: instruction, feedback, reward. Then you manage the boss so that you both get what you want.

If managing the boss doesn't work for you, it's time to leave.

Managing the boss works. I have consulted with thousands of people who have proved it.

But sometimes you may not be able to adapt or to manage the boss well enough to be able to enjoy your job and perform at the expected level. If managing the boss doesn't work for you, it's time to leave.

Jeff came to that conclusion — reluctantly. A marketing executive, he made a tremendous effort to adapt to the needs of his boss and the demands of his work environment. He wanted to see if he could change his behavior permanently and be happy in his current position. At the very least, he knew he needed to buy time while he straightened out his personal life. He gave it a heck of a try, and I respect him for that. Then, when he felt he could adapt no further, and his problems on the home front had stabilized, he had the courage to give up a plum job and the golden handcuffs that went with it to seek real happiness in his career.

Jeff was an *Innovator*, a strategic planner in a Fortune 50 company. The executive he reported to was an *Abdicator* boss. A perfect match. Jeff reacted quickly, changed rapidly, and took a lot of license with company policy. He was impatient with the *Implementers* around him who seemed slow moving to him and he yelled at them to get them moving.

The boss didn't object to Jeff's impatient behavior. He didn't flinch when Jeff fired someone with whom he had no patience. He didn't get ruffled when Jeff pulled advertising that a customer survey said wasn't working and used a totally untested advertisement in its place. He didn't try to change Jeff. After all, he was an *Abdicator*, and he frankly respected Jeff's style.

But the company was something else. The work environment was clearly *Directive*. The boss had long ago adapted to the company style as an employee. As a boss, he enjoyed this renegade under him — until people began to go over the boss' head to complain about Jeff. Then Jeff's style became a problem for him. Being an

Abdicator boss, Jeff's superior wasn't about to coach him into being someone different. But, to solve the problem, he did arrange for Jeff to be transferred to another department with another supervisor, a true *Coach* boss.

Thus Jeff went from the right boss in the wrong environment to the wrong boss in the wrong environment. Needless to say, he was unhappy. So was his new boss. But at least the new *Coach* boss, unlike the *Abdicator* boss, was willing to tell him what he was doing wrong and teach him to do better. That is why the boss sent him to me for executive coaching.

Among other assessments, I gave him *The Mulling Factor*. I showed him what his preferred style was as an *Innovator* and what kind of boss and environment he needed to be productive and happy. I helped him see what he would have to do to satisfy and manage his current boss and to fit in with the *Directive* environment of his company.

I must add that this was also a traumatic time in Jeff's personal life. His mother was slowly dying that year; his son was recalcitrant at home and had been having disciplinary problems at school. He and his wife disagreed on what had gone wrong and what to do about it. Their discord was so great that his wife had threatened to leave. He expected she would take their young daughter with her and leave him to handle the son's situation by himself. Facing loss on all fronts, the last thing he wanted to do right then was go out and find a new job.

In addition, Jeff had stock options and great health insurance that he might have to use for his son; his own blood pressure had leapt into the unhealthy range. Leaving was not an option ... unless ... and this was what he dreaded ... they asked him to leave. Jeff could see right away that he was dangerously close to being asked to leave. I understood his need to stay with the company. He and I both saw that for him to stay and just endure would be a short-lived proposition. He wouldn't last a month. Doing nothing was out. Therefore, I showed him what his options were — either to adapt temporarily while he determined if he could learn to manage his boss on a permanent basis, or to look for a new job now. Remember, Jeff was mismatched by two whole types of employee style. A difficult leap. But because of his circumstances he was highly motivated to try.

He learned how to be helpful to his boss and less competitive with others. He learned to give his boss what he wanted. He learned to check rules before acting and to follow the company pecking order. He asked to have meetings with his boss once a week. He learned to accept the people around him who were less flexible and less independent than he, and who, in fact were meeting the company's needs better. Jeff didn't enjoy his new restrictions, but he was less

> I can give you a six-word formula for success: Think things through — then follow through. **Captain Edward V. Rickenbacker**

stressed because people liked him better and got off his back.

As time went on, Jeff's boss, like a good coach, continued his education. He tried to teach Jeff to delegate, to share information and take the time to inform others instead of being overly independent.

I figured that Jeff had made the transition from *Innovator* to *Participator*-type behavior; he was still not the *Implementer* he needed to be in this job, but the boss had also adapted some too. I admired Jeff's determination and persistence, and I supported him in his new role. It's not often that someone successfully makes a leap of two styles as shown in **The Mulling Factor**.

But Jeff was still misemployed. And so it didn't surprise me when, about a year later, Jeff came to me and said things had stabilized in his personal life. And that at work he was doing okay, but he realized he was not being himself. It was a stretch for him to do well in this job and that what he really wanted to do, now that the pressure was off, was to find that ideal job that I had talked about.

A very specific moment of truth had brought Jeff to this decision. He had given some information about a strategy to a senior vice president, but left out key information he assumed the senior vice president would know. The senior vice president used the information in a public presentation and was eaten alive.

"I figured he knew that!" Jeff protested. "After all, he's a senior vice president; he's supposed to know some things on his own." In response to the catastrophe, Jeff's long-suffering boss met with him and, in true *Coach* fashion, instituted a new procedure: when you report information to the executives that are your internal clients, you will put it on a form, and you will fill out all the blanks on the form.

Jeff took one look at the form, which resembled a grade school teacher's lesson plan, and he *It takes courage* rebelled. He was not about to fill out forms for *to leave.* senior vice presidents. He considered that requirement insulting to him and to the other executives. He told his boss he would study it, and he took it back to his office.

Soon Jeff was conducting a job search where his needs, according to his **Mulling Factor** type, would be fully met. It was not long before he left his job on his own terms and went with a small advertising firm, an *Entrepreneurial* environment where change is rapid, and the latest idea is king. He has ten clients at a time instead of the one internal client — his company — that he had before. He can be very creative and take risks. In the "you-win-some, you-lose-some" attitude of the company, if one ad campaign doesn't succeed and he loses a customer, he gets a new one.

The key to this success story was courage, strength, and the insight gained by using **The Mulling Factor** as a quide.

When It's Time To Leave

It takes courage to leave. I know that. But what does it take to face years of stress and dissatisfaction at your job? Endurance. Which is better, to have courage now and look forward to happiness for years to come in your future jobs or to have enormous endurance to face years of dissatisfaction and stress — and possible termination?

My experience consulting thousands of mis-employed professionals convinces me that it's not a problem to make a change in your thirties, forties, fifties, or even sixties.

Believe you can make a successful change. All it takes is the commitment of time and effort to make the change as an informed "consumer."

CHAPTER SEVEN

Beyond the Snow Job to the Right Job

You don't need to be misemployed! You can be in control.

> We've entered an era when very good, competent people aren't getting jobs. One remedy is to stand out, to self-promote. If you do, you're going to get the nod over some co-worker.
>
> **Jeffrey P. Davidson**

IT'S TIME TO MAKE YOUR MOVE. Maybe you've managed your boss successfully, reaped the benefits, and gotten all you wanted out of your current job. Maybe your boss just couldn't be managed. Maybe it was too late because your mismatch had "gotten personal." Maybe you didn't even try because you were already discouraged by all the hassles and headaches. Or, simply because the prospect of finally having "the right job" was something you couldn't resist.

Whatever the reason, you're now ready to use all you've learned. This time you're going to get it right. Not only the right money and the right work, but, thanks to *The Mulling Factor*, the right boss and the right work environment.

I don't want to make it sound easy. It's not. It's still going to take careful planning and hard work to get that dream job. But this time you know exactly what you're seeking. You're not shooting in the dark. You won't be wasting your energy or settling for misemployment. In fact, you may even enjoy the process this time because you're going to be in control. Every step of the way.

Don't stop asking questions.

Put Your Ear To The Ground

Start with an overview of potential companies. Ask around. Attend professional meetings, industry social events, and civic gatherings. See who knows something, perhaps inside information, about the companies in which you are interested. Better than asking, "What do you hear about X company?" ask your contacts in the industry to compare three or four of their competitors without telling them that you're especially interested in one of them. This is the best way to get impressions of the company and how it is viewed in the community or in the industry. Ask questions like, "How would you compare the management in these companies?" Or, "How effective is their R&D (or marketing or quality control or whatever concerns you)?"

For general information on a public company, ask the company for a copy of a 10-K, a document that all public companies must submit

A prudent question is one-half of wisdom.
Francis Bacon

annually to the Securities and Exchange Commission, or download the document from the Internet <www.sec.gov>. The 10-K tells you the company's major competitors, the pitfalls it faces, potential mergers or acquisitions, compensation of senior officers, and so forth, all information not usually found in the annual report. Also, research a public company at <www.quicken.com>.

For a private company, it's much harder to get useful information. A good source would be <www.hoovers.com>. A Dun & Bradstreet report could be helpful; ask your friends in finance to help you get one. Search Internet databases by industry, company size, geographic region, etc. Look for clues (and interview topics) in press releases <www.prnewswire.com>, or at <www.bizjournals.com>.

Make good use of the Internet.

For official information, check company homepages. Try <www.companyname.com> or <www.associationname.org> or call the company directly and ask for their Internet address.

In addition, *The Mulling Companies* maintains a web page on the Internet with useful information on job hunting including addresses for search engines, job bulletin boards, newspaper classifieds, headhunters, salary comparison data, and links to our favorite web sites. Check us out at <www.mulling.com>, Resource Center, Favorite Internet Sites.

Narrowing The Field
— You Are an Interviewer Also

You've targeted a few companies because of industry or reputation, and you've asked all the associates from your professional and personal network for leads. You've custom-designed your resume for the new job you want and polished it so it stands out in the crowd.

Now you're ready to call your most promising contacts and send them your resume. You're ready for interviews.

Mindset is everything. Remember you are interviewing as well as being interviewed. You're not a horse being examined at a horse market. Evaluation works both ways. While the company wants to know if you are the right person for the job, you're going to determine if this is the right job for you.

Your first interview may not be with the boss but with a "gatekeeper," a Human Resources specialist whose job is to screen applicants. Here are the typical stages in the interview process.

Mindset is everything.

> Everything comes to he who hustles while he waits.
> **Thomas Edison**

The Gatekeeper Plus 3

STEPS	GOALS
Gatekeeper	Get by the screening process, meet qualifications, get invited back
Interview # 1 with the boss	Create good chemistry, get invited back
Interview # 2 with the boss	Discuss the work and skill requirements, get invited back
Interview #3 with the boss	Confirm job fit, get offer, negotiate salary

Know the gatekeeper and what role they play.

There's nothing terribly wrong with this order of business as far as it goes, but I'm going to modify and enlarge the format from one that will get you a job to one that will get you the right job.

Getting by the Gate

The gatekeeper tells you something you need to know about the work environment. In a bureaucratic environment, the gatekeeper has more power; in an entrepreneurial environment, the gatekeeper has less, or more likely, there will be no gatekeeper. You'll talk to the boss herself. The gatekeeper is not as interested in "chemistry" as the actual boss will be, so how you get along with the gatekeeper may not matter as much. Instead, the gatekeeper will have the requirements for the job and will be looking for how well you meet a narrow profile. If you don't meet these requirements exactly, you will probably not be invited back for another interview.

You, however, may think you are suited for a certain job even without the exact credentials. You may be missing some required skill or experience; but, either it's a skill you can easily learn, or you've had some other experience which may prove more valuable to the company than the one that's missing. If you could just talk to the boss, you figure you could convince him you're the one he wants. You can mention your unique qualifications to the gatekeeper, but it may not help; the gatekeeper usually is not empowered to make judgments outside of the qualifications. Your special charms will be wasted here.

So it's definitely better to by-pass the gatekeeper and go directly to the boss. Accomplish this by getting in personal contact with the boss and arranging an interview without going through the Human Resources department. Here's where your networking helps. Find someone who knows the boss or a boss at the company you're pursuing. Ask if you may use their name when calling for an appointment. Then you can open your conversation with: "Jeff Allen suggested I call you." It's even better if good old Jeff calls the prospective boss and puts in a good word for you before you make the call. If the boss agrees to an interview, don't worry about the

Human Resources procedures. If the boss wants you, in all but the most bureaucratic environments, the boss will send you back through Human Resources with his own weighty stamp of approval.

Interview # 1 with the Boss

After you've gotten by or around the gatekeeper, the objective of the first interview with the prospective boss is to get invited back for a second interview. This is a matter of establishing chemistry between you and the boss so that, as he narrows his choice of candidates, you're on the short list.

Be a good listener and observer.

Personality does count. You want to see if there's chemistry between you and the boss. Look for a personal connection.

Look around the boss' office. One keen observation is worth a thousand words of interviewing. Is the desk neat? Is it cluttered? Does the boss have pictures of his family? Golf trophies? Diplomas? A bust of Winston Churchill? Personal items tell you what is important to the boss. If you relate to any of these, say so.

"Oh, you play golf. Where did you win this one? … Oh, I played there once when I was a second string walk-on."

Or, nodding to Churchill's bust, you say, "Great leader! Last year I visited Chartwell, his country estate in Kent."

As you get into your interview, take your lead from the boss. Let his questions drive the interview.

If he says, "I see you're from Penn State. I think you have one of the best coaches in football," then you have a clue to where his interests lie. Pursue the subject.

If, noting an item on your resume, he says, "That's a job I did for a while. I know what that's like," he's defining what he thinks is important. Following his lead makes it easier to connect. He cares about your background — and his. You can ask questions like: "How long have you been at Acme Company?" or "What was your previous position there?" or "In what position did you start with this company?" and, "What experience did you have before that?"

Let the **Mulling Factor** *go to work for you.*

If, however, you have trouble getting a conversation going with the boss, remember that a lot of managers are uncomfortable interviewing; it's their least favorite activity. Prepare some questions to help the boss along, to help him interview you. Anything you can do to make the interviewer comfortable the more likely you are to get the second interview.

Sometimes the boss likes you so much that he makes you an offer on the first interview. Don't accept on the spot. The quick offer may mean the company is desperate or that they don't want or know how to thoroughly explore the fit between you and the company. Or the boss just

> True enjoyment comes from activity of the mind and exercise of the body; the two are ever united.
> **Humboldt**

doesn't want to do any more interviewing. Say, "I appreciate the offer and I'm very interested. I'd like to think about it overnight and get back together tomorrow."

You got to the boss, and you hit it off! Now you have it made. You talk to him two more times; and if you both still like what you see, you get a job (and they get an employee).

Whoa! If it's so easy, why have so many people interviewed the boss three times and then been misemployed? Because they didn't know about *The Mulling Factor*. But you do. Finding the right job is going to be easier for you. Knowing what you know about your needs, you're going to do more investigating than the typical job seeker. And your Interview # 2 with the boss is going to be a lot more productive than the less informed job seekers' interview would be.

Interview # 2 with the Boss —Asking the Revealing Questions

The second interview with the boss typically revolves around the work you may be doing. You'll discuss in more detail what your duties would be and the skills and experience you have in these areas. The work is important, of course. Remember that the right work is one of the elements of the ideal job (and the easiest to evaluate). But what is even more important? The right boss and the right work environment. Therefore, you'll be exploring far beyond the work at this interview. You'll be trying to determine the type of boss this person is by observing and listening well and by asking questions that reveal his supervisory style and the type of work environment of the position.

You'll use the discussion of the work to find out the boss' approach to the work. As he lists work items and goals, ask:

- "What does the work look like when it's done well?"

- "What does the work look like when it's done poorly?"

- "What aspects of the work do you see as the most important?"

All of these questions lead toward *The Mulling Factor*. You'll want to address each of your needs as identified by *The Mulling Factor*. As a reminder, take out the Chart 3 on page 112-113 and look at the words that describe your Best Boss and Best Work Environment. The object of the second interview is to determine if your prospective boss is one you want, and if the work environment sounds like the best one for you.

Don't just take the characteristics on the list and ask the boss if she has them. All the phrases on the chart are neutral or favorable, and if

Are you
interviewing
the boss?

you ask "Are you supportive?" or "Are you empowering?" the boss may say, "Yes." This may sometimes be deliberately deceptive, but usually it's a difference of perspective. What the boss may see as "support," you may see as control or neglect. You don't want to guide her or give away the answers you are seeking; you want to see what comes naturally to her mind.

If you're an *Implementer*, you're looking for a *Coach*. The chart tells you this is someone who teaches and directs. Don't ask your prospective boss, "Are you someone who teaches and directs?" Ask instead, "Do you feel that developing your staff is part of your role?" If the answer is "Yes," ask, "How do you do it?"

Similarly, if you're an *Innovator*, don't ask, "What is your theory of empowering people?" Ask instead, "Do you have a hands-on or hands-off style?" or, even more neutral, "How do you describe your management style?" When he answers, ask, "Could you give an example of how you'd manage someone this way?" His answer gives you an idea of what "hands-on" and "hands-off" mean to him.

Here's another way to see if the boss fits your **Mulling Factor** description of the ideal boss. Instead of asking a general question, make up an example: "If you give me a new project to explore, initiate, and implement (be as specific as you can for your industry), how do you want to be informed of my progress?" Or, "If one of my subordinates was at odds with another one and, in fact, seemed to be sabotaging the other's efforts, how much involvement would you want to have with the problem and at what point? Or would you expect me to handle it alone?" Sometimes people can answer behavioral questions like these more readily than they can answer abstract questions.

Before the end of the interview, you should have a good idea what kind of boss the one you're interviewing is or, at least, the kind he thinks he is or wishes he were. And, at this point, the boss also knows enough about you that he may offer you a job.

If you get an offer at this meeting, don't accept the job and don't talk about money at this time — no matter how positive you're feeling. Instead, say, "I'm really interested in the job, but may I ask a few questions to be sure there is a good fit for you and for me?"

Since the boss' view or representation of himself and the job may not be accurate, you need to explore further. Ask your prospective boss to allow you to observe your potential department or work team in action so you get a realistic view of the job. You also need his help in contacting the following people:

Employment or misemployment: their both in your hands.

The "A" List

- The person you would be replacing, for example, your predecessor
- The boss' employees, your future peers
- The clients or customers, whether internal or external
- The boss' boss

Sometimes when I show this list to job candidates, I get a grimace or a wince as a response. So go ahead and wince. But you risk misemployment if you don't talk to some, if not all, of the people on this list. Which is worse, asking these questions or accepting the wrong job? If you need convincing, let me tell you one more cautionary tale.

The Last Cautionary Tale

Morris was an *Innovator* looking for a very senior position in marketing. He interviewed with the president of a company who said he wanted a strong person to set up new marketing programs and to redefine the whole function of

MORRIS' HIGHEST SCORE:			
Innovator			
A	B	C	D
23	42	62	(73)

the marketing department. "New programs" and "redefining functions" was Morris' kind of language. So Morris signed on for a $300,000 package. What he did not do was interview anyone except the boss himself. Morris met a few other people, and several of them interviewed HIM, but he didn't interview THEM on the things that count.

It turned out the president was not at all the *Abdicator* boss that Morris thought he was. He was, in fact, a *Coach*. The president didn't trust Morris to initiate programs or changes on his own. Moreover, he was not even in favor of making the changes or investing the money in the new direction — he would have preferred an *Implementer* marketing executive to do his bidding to decide if the programs were too expensive. There was no way Morris could succeed at the goals for which he thought he had been employed. He eventually discovered that those new programs had been the parent company's idea, not the president's. Without the necessary financial support and authority, Morris could make no progress in a new direction. The parent company, giving up on improving their return on investment in that subsidiary, cut back by eliminating forty positions, including his.

Why didn't Morris realize this president didn't give his executives anything like the free rein an *Innovator* needs? For one thing, in his interview, he wasn't looking for his *Mulling*

> My job is never work — the only time it seems like work is when I'd rather be doing something else.
> **Source Unknown**

Factor characteristics. For another, he didn't ask the appropriate people who could have told him what he needed to know? I would have gone to the departing marketing executive; then the boss' boss at the parent company; next, the executives at Morris' level in other departments. The moral of the story is: don't YOU fail to get information about the prospective boss and the work environment from the boss' colleagues, subordinates, and superiors.

Watch out for intimidation and know how you will handle it.

Be a Wise Consumer

I often ask people in my seminars how many of them would be too intimidated to ask for the names of these sources or permission to interview them. About half of them admit they would be intimidated. If you're in that half, I'm going to try to get you over your timidity!

There are four very good reasons why you shouldn't feel awkward asking to interview the people who have worked with and for your prospective boss.

First, remember that your prospective boss and the company's Human Resources people are going to be asking questions about you. They're going to check your references and maybe look at your credit record and even your driving record. Why shouldn't you do the same? You have every right to investigate them as thoroughly and per-

sonally as they do you. Just do it with the profes-
sionalism I am recommending in this chapter.

Second, in taking (or turning down) a job
offer, you're about to make a decision that
involves tens of thousands, if not hundreds of
thousands of dollars over a year's time. Think
what you'd do about any other decision involving
an equal amount of money. If you were buying a
house, you'd do a lot more than open all the clos-
et doors, look for signs of moisture in the base-
ment, and check out the furnace. You'd also have
the house appraised and inspected, and you'd
have a title search and legal survey. If you were
buying a previously owned car for a fraction of
your annual salary, you'd look at the service
records, have the car checked over by an independent mechanic, and test drive it at different
speeds. Wouldn't you think someone was foolish
who didn't look into these things for such a
major purchase?

The third reason for being comfortable
investigating your prospective job through a
variety of sources is that your prospective
employer, in fact, should be favorably impressed
that you're so thorough and knowledgeable in
your investigation. Because of your questions,
your prospective employer should look forward
to your using the same good skills on their company's behalf. And do you want to go to work for
a company that seems to be hiding some of their

Know the company you are interviewing before you get in front of the interviewers.

sources? They want to hire a wise consumer. Wouldn't you?

And fourth, the company you're considering should be happy you are doing all this work to achieve a good fit because every mismatch hurts them, too. Mismatches cause lower productivity, missed opportunity and the expense of rehiring and retraining. You're doing the company a favor by doing their job for them.

Putting Words in Your Mouth

Be prepared and don't be afraid to ask questions.

To help you ask your prospective boss, diplomatically, for other sources of information about the job you're considering, here are some samples of specific language you can use.

To reach the person you're replacing:

Who is doing this job now?

- *If the answer is "no one":* Why is the position being created?

- *If already gone:* Why did she leave? Where did she go to work after leaving your company? Then call her at the company to discuss the circumstances around her departure.

To reach current employees:

Do you mind if I talk to some of the people in the department to insure I am a good fit with my future co-workers?

To reach clients, internal and external:

- Who are some of your major clients with whom I would be working?

- *If you had been in the same industry previously:* A good bit of our business came from the Ajax Company. Do you do business with them?

- *If clients are internal:* Who do you interact with the most, or who would I be interacting with the most?

- Who is the user of your department's services? To insure a smooth transition, would it be possible for me to talk to them?

To reach the boss' boss:

- Who do you report to?

- Would it be beneficial for me to talk to your boss? It certainly may be good to have his input on my hiring.

- *To a noncommittal answer:* When would it be possible?

If the boss refuses to give you contact information or tries to discourage you from talking to any of these sources, beware. An uncooperative response is a red flag that there is a problem here. If your prospective boss says, "Oh, I don't think that will be necessary," you definitely want to pursue the matter.

In fact, when faced with reluctance to offer contact with sources, you now add a "B" List to your total list of people to interview: former employees of the boss in this company, former customers and clients, even former employees of the boss in his previous company or position, and, especially, vendors who deal with your boss' counterparts in many different companies. All of these sources will have a different prospective from those on the "A" List, and they may be more open in discussing the boss and the work environment you're investigating.

Here's how to reach these sources:

The "B" List

To reach former employees, ask the Human Resources department:

- What has been the rate of turnover in the department?

- Why did they leave this position?

- To insure I am the best fit for this position, if I am given just one name, do you mind if I talk to them?

To reach former clients or customers, ask the boss or his employees:

- Have you ever lost a client?

- If so, who was it?

- What do you think the problem was and how can I help to repair the damage?

- You can also ask former employees to refer you to other clients or customers.

To reach employees of the boss at a previous company:

- You have already asked the boss where he worked previously. Call the boss' former department directly.

Watch out for red flags.

At the end of this second interview, schedule a date for the third meeting far enough in the future to give you time to interview the other people on your lists.

Your Checklist Between Interview # 2 and Interview # 3

And what are you trying to learn from all these interviews with your prospective boss' associates? You're trying to learn if the boss and the work environment fit your needs as identified by *The Mulling Factor*.

For each of your new contacts, simply rephrase the questions you asked the boss until you have covered all of your needs. For example, "How does he develop his employees?" and "Is his management style hands-off or hands-on?" Asking parallel questions of the boss and of his associates helps you compare answers readily.

Other questions like, "Does he give you all you need to get the job done?" taps the unique employee perspective.

Don't expect the answers to be the same. The boss probably is not trying to be dishonest. He has a continuum in mind of hands-on and hands-off. For example, he may think he is in the middle; that is, not too hands-on, not too hands-off, but just right. Your other sources may have a different continuum in mind based on their experience with bosses. If, however, there is a sizable discrepancy between the boss' self-assessment and his associates' assessment on a particular point, this could be a red flag. You want to explore the issue more fully.

The Boss' Boss
— a Special Kind of Interview

The interview with the boss' boss is special for several reasons. One, it is the most intimidating. That means you have to prepare extra well so you don't waste her time. Two, the interview is very important because she's very important. You may work for her sooner or later. She's in a position to support you in any disagreement or crisis. She may ask for you to be promoted.

The boss' boss is big; therefore, you need to ask her big questions. You must choose questions that capitalize on her perspective, which could be entirely different from that of her employee, your prospective boss.

Here are some examples:

* "Where do you see the company (the division) going and what is this department's role?" or "Where do you see the department going and what would my role be?"

* "What has been the track record of the department's recent performance?"

* If she expresses disappointment in an area: "What do you feel is the best approach to solve this problem?" and "What degree of involvement will Mr. B. have in solving this?"

* If you are talking about changes that have occurred or the boss wants to occur, ask: "What role do you see Mr. B. having in these changes?"

* "Has there been a lot of turnover at my level?" If so, "Why do you think this is so?"

You want to know if the boss' boss sees the work the same as the boss does. What does success represent to her? Does the boss' boss think you'll get the support you need for the job.

Remember: bosses are employees too.

Two Sides of the Coin

WARNING! Your boss is often an employee as well as a boss. You must seek to determine your boss' style as a **boss**, not his **employee** style used to report to his own boss. Your prospective boss may be an *Innovator*, constantly forging new ground as an employee. That does not mean he is a boss who wants *Innovators* to report to him.

Do you think General Douglas MacArthur, an *Innovator*, wanted a lot of creative people with ideas of their own to carry out his plan? NO, he wanted people who hit the beach when he said hit the beach, no questions asked. If they survived, someday they might get to develop their own strategies, but not in MacArthur's war.

And, did Michelangelo want his assistants to develop their own style while working on the Sistine Chapel — a little impressionist here and a little cubist over there? NO, he wanted *Conformers* with great technical skill but who would color inside the lines and paint by the numbers. As in the case of MacArthur's soldiers, their creativity would have to wait for another day.

When you're trying to determine what kind of boss your prospective supervisor is, don't be misled by what type of employee the boss himself or the boss' boss says he is; consider more pertinent the type of boss his employees say he is. And notice that the prospective boss may also talk to you with his "employee" hat on. It's his management style you are trying to discover, not his employee style.

A Parking Lot With A View

In addition to interviewing people for their individual perspectives, also try out a new perspective yourself: go through the motion of going to work at your prospective company. Make the drive in the morning, sit in the parking lot and watch the employees arriving for work. While visiting the reception area and having lunch in the cafeteria during the interview process, you'll get a feel for the company and its work environment by watching the people who work for the company. Look around and ask yourself, "Do I want to be one of these people?"

Interview # 3 With The Boss —Exploring Inconsistencies

The third interview is to confirm your findings from interviews with others and to iron out any inconsistencies you may have discovered. Come into this interview with a tentative sense of the boss' type and the inconsistencies that keep your conclusions from being certain. Now you'll confirm your tentative impression or change it.

Be honest — not confrontive. If you've discovered inconsistencies, it's essential that you straighten it out. Confirm your *Mulling Factor* conclusions.

"I've got a pretty consistent reading from the staff that …." (State the information that contradicts the boss' perspective as he expressed it to you.)

About a feeling that the boss himself is misemployed or at odds with his boss, ask: "What priority do you feel for this initiative?" or "I have a strong feeling, Ms. C. (the boss' boss) *really* wants this to change. Do you agree?"

In your attempts to get a true picture of the boss and the environment as it relates to your needs, you'll get a gut feeling that says this is the job for you … or not.

If you feel this is the job for you, now is the time to engage in salary negotiations. If you've built a strong rapport, have the qualifications, and your needs as an employee fit the supervisory style of your boss and the company, you may get more money than that first-interview offer would have been.

Now that I've expanded the interview process, here's the new flow:

Interviewing
— The New Expanded Format

STEPS	GOALS
Gatekeeper	Go around or get through, get invited to meet the boss
Interview # 1 with the boss	Create good chemistry, begin to assess the boss' style, get invited back
Interview # 2 with the boss	Discuss the work, skills, ask questions about the boss' management style and the work environment, ask for permission to observe work and to interview others
Between Interviews # 1 and # 2	Observe work, observe environment, interview "A" list of associates and, if necessary, "B" list
Interview #3 with the boss	Confirm, discuss discrepancies, consider offer, negotiate salary

We can chart our future clearly and wisely only when we know the path which has led to the present.
Adlai E. Stevenson

It is not uncommon for three interviews to be held on the same day, especially if you have come from out of town. One of them will be with the boss and the other two with associates. Ask the two associates the same questions you ask the boss and any others that interest you. It

Build your confidence and let it work for you.

will be harder for you to process the answers and comments and develop new questions in the abbreviated format. However, knowing the long process will help you prepare and react successfully.

These steps and lists of questions may seem tedious or overkill. However, the work you do with a focus on *The Mulling Factor* is much more rewarding than going through the motions without a purpose. You will know what to ask and what your target is. As you take each step and reach your objective, you build confidence. You perceive the respect the boss and others have for your insight and persistence. That respect also builds confidence. And confidence brings a better chance of good chemistry and ultimate success.

And finally, with people changing jobs every few years, you will become proficient at this novel approach to the process. This will serve you well to be able to repeat this for your next job search. This procedure is the most security you will have in the workforce today. Being a wiser consumer has its advantages.

CHAPTER EIGHT

And Now ... It's in Your Hands

NOW YOU HAVE all the information you need. You know if you're misemployed and why. You know what you can do about it. And you know the specific steps on the road to happy, productive employment.

In other words, with the help of *The Mulling Factor*, you can now be a wise consumer in the world of work.

But all I can give you is information. I can't give you motivation. I can tell you this: information without the courage to act on it is useless. And I can't give you courage. I wish I could.

What I can assure you is that the approach outlined in this book works. It has worked for thousands of people, and I believe it will work for you. It worked for Wesley, who started out with the same fears that you may have. Maybe you should hear him tell his own story:

"I really didn't like my job. There was something about my boss I didn't like at all. I avoided him or played along with him because it was safer. But there were times when I rebelled.

The job really was depressing. Over the years, I applied for higher positions in other areas in our company. All the applications had to go through my boss. He wouldn't even consider me for these jobs, saying I didn't meet the criteria.

The problem was that once years before, at a management weekend retreat, all the managers were given a profile test to see if they were right-brained or left-brained. They were looking for examples of the extremes and my scores showed the most extreme left-brained functioning in the group. Everyone there, my peers and my superiors, knew that I was off the scale as left-brained. Their idea was that the good leader is in the exact center. Okay, I'm highly analytical, so what do I do now? I've tried to take action to be more right-brained. I've taken the test three times and I'm still left-brained. Consequently, I've gotten pigeon-holed as not having the potential to rise in management. They will not even consider me.

About a year ago, I began to look for a job out-side the company, but I went about it all wrong and I didn't get any offers. I was feeling more and more depressed. I got to the point of "I give up. Fire me if you want."

They did, and I went through a whirl of differ-ent emotions. When they called me in, it was very painful. This is the way it was put to me: that they were trying to change my position to be more global, and I didn't have the skills to do that.

But when I walked out the door, I actually breathed a great sigh of relief that it was final-ly over. Another feeling was anger. I wanted to punch that manager.

At the same time, I felt very optimistic. I figured with my knowledge and experience, it wouldn't be very difficult to get another job, not just another job, but a better job.

Part of the severance package was to use The Mulling Companies for outplacement. I thought all they would give me was a desk, a chair, and a phone. I wasn't expecting career focus and training in things like interviewing. That was the biggest surprise.

One day a consultant put **The Mulling Factor** *on my desk and said, "Please take it in the next day or so." It took about fifteen minutes.*

Later, Emory Mulling explained what **The Mulling Factor** *meant and went over the scoring. That's when a light bulb flashed.*

The Mulling Factor *helped explain why I had not gotten along with my boss. After all those years, I finally understood my boss and had a better picture of who I was. I wasn't just a left-brain with no leadership capabilities. When I looked at the categories, it explained why he did certain things and why I reacted the way I did. When I understood what* **The Mulling Factor** *said to me, it relieved my anger against my boss.*

I really think that **The Mulling Factor***, as compared to other career assessments I've taken, gives useful answers and information beyond all others. It tells you not just who you are but what you need from management and the work environment. Nothing else does that. The others tell you if you're left-brained or right-brained or a people-person or an introvert, but then what do you do with the infromation?*

Now I've had interviews with several companies and I'm expecting an offer from one of them. I've been flown to the home office where I

Don't give up! Don't settle.

Fall seven times, stand up eight.
Japanese Proverb

interviewed three people, and I've had several follow-up conversations by phone.

In these interviews, I'm using any analytical skills to my advantage. I've been asking the boss and others there about the boss' management style and the company's work environment. People understand perfectly well what I'm asking. They seem to answer honestly. They're not withholding information. I know what I'm seeking, what my needs are. More than anything, I know what kind of person won't be a good boss for me.

If I get an offer from this company, I'll take it because it's exactly the job I want, and I think I'm exactly the kind of guy they want."

—Wesley

> There are two primary choices in life: to accept conditions as they exist, or accept the responsibility for changing them.
> **Dr. Denis Waitley**

I have every respect for Wesley. He has been strong enough to learn and committed enough to take the time to investigate companies and jobs until he found several where he would fit. He got the job he wanted, and I congratulate him.

There was a reason you started reading this book, and a reason you've stuck with it all the way to the end. You want something better for yourself as a worker. You're not willing to settle;

you're not ready to stop searching for your perfect job.

Your instinct is correct

What I want to tell you is that your instinct is right: you don't have to settle for the wrong job. You shouldn't stop your search. You can have the successful, happy life you want and deserve.

Reading this book is your first step toward that life. Now that you have the information you need, that missing piece in the job search puzzle, you can take the next steps with confidence. My work with thousands of people like you confirms my belief that happiness at work is not only a possibility, but an obligation. And with the help of *The Mulling Factor*, not only a possibility, but a probability. Please trust me.

Better yet, trust yourself.

**If you found this book thought provoking …
If you are interested in having this author …
or other of our consulting authors
design a workshop or seminar for your
company, organization, school, or team …**

Let the experienced and knowledgeable group of experts at
The Diogenes Consortium go to work for you.
With literally hundreds of years of combined
experience in:

*Human Resources • Employee Retention
Management • Pro-Active Leadership • Teams
Encouragement • Empowerment • Motivation
Energizing • Delegating Responsibility
Spirituality in the Workplace
Presentations to start-ups and Fortune 100 companies,
tax-exempt organizations and schools
(public and private, elementary through university)
religious groups and organizations*

**Call today for a list of our
authors/speakers/presenters/consultants**

Call toll free at 866-602-1476
Or write to us at:
2445 River Tree Circle
Sanford, FL 32771